W9-BCB-310

NEW DIRECTIONS FOR INSTITUTIONAL RESEARCH

Patrick T. Terenzini, *The Pennsylvania State University*
EDITOR-IN-CHIEF

Analyzing Faculty Workload

Jon F. Wergin
Virginia Commonwealth University

EDITOR

NUMBER 83, FALL 1994

JOSSEY-BASS PUBLISHERS
San Francisco

ANALYZING FACULTY WORKLOAD
Jon F. Wergin (ed.)
New Directions for Institutional Research, no. 83
Volume XVI, Number 3
Patrick T. Terenzini, Editor-in-Chief

Microfilm copies of issues and articles are available in 16mm and 35mm, as well as microfiche in 105mm, through University Microfilms Inc., 300 North Zeeb Road, Ann Arbor, Michigan 48106-1346.

LC 85-645339   ISSN 0271-0579   ISBN 0-7879-9988-1

NEW DIRECTIONS FOR INSTITUTIONAL RESEARCH is part of The Jossey-Bass Higher and Adult Education Series and is published quarterly by Jossey-Bass Inc., Publishers, 350 Sansome Street, San Francisco, California 94104-1342 (publication number USPS 098-830). Second-class postage paid at San Francisco, California, and at additional mailing offices. POST-MASTER: Send address changes to New Directions for Institutional Research, Jossey-Bass Inc., Publishers, 350 Sansome Street, San Francisco, California 94104-1342.

SUBSCRIPTIONS for 1994 cost $47.00 for individuals and $62.00 for institutions, agencies, and libraries.

EDITORIAL CORRESPONDENCE should be sent to the editor-in-chief, Patrick T. Terenzini, Center for the Study of Higher Education, The Pennsylvania State University, 403 South Allen Street, Suite 104, University Park, Pennsylvania 16801-5202.

Photograph of the library by Michael Graves at San Juan Capistrano by Chad Slattery © 1984. All rights reserved.

Manufactured in the United States of America. Nearly all Jossey-Bass books, jackets, and periodicals are printed on recycled paper that contains at least 50 percent recycled waste, including 10 percent postconsumer waste. Many of our materials are also printed with vegetable-based inks; during the printing process, these inks emit fewer volatile organic compounds (VOCs) than petroleum-based inks. VOCs contribute to the formation of smog.

THE ASSOCIATION FOR INSTITUTIONAL RESEARCH was created in 1966 to benefit, assist, and advance research leading to improved understanding, planning, and operation of institutions of higher education. Publication policy is set by its Publications Board.

For information about the Association for Institutional Research, write to the following address:

AIR Executive Office
314 Stone Building
Florida State University
Tallahassee, FL 32306-3038

(904) 644-4470

CONTENTS

EDITOR'S NOTES

External pressures for change in higher education are perhaps stronger now than at any time in the last fifty years. Budget problems, once regarded as cyclical, now appear structural, and thus refuse to go away. What we see in state after state are permanent reductions in state support for higher education: average state support in 1992 and 1993 declined in real dollars for two years in a row, for the first time in history. One analyst has estimated that total capital renewal and replacement costs at our colleges and universities now reach $60 billion, about half of annual operating costs for all institutions! Smaller budgets are likely to continue throughout the 1990s, and may shrink more, even as the national economy improves.

How did we get to such a state of affairs? Higher education in this country has lost what Robert Zemsky (1991) calls its "academic sanctuary"—its exalted status as an unexamined good. Reasons for this grim scenario are primarily political. Spiraling college tuition (the method most institutions have chosen to deal with their budget deficits) outpaces even medical costs; an increasingly sophisticated public is getting more and more skeptical of the value of a college education; the press has taken delight in seizing on its vulnerabilities—all these changes have led to a broad public consensus that higher education has simply lost its way. College faculty in particular have borne the brunt of the criticism. We are sheltered, spoiled folk with cushy jobs, the perception goes; we probably don't work very hard, and if we do, we're more interested in narrow, inaccessible scholarship than in work that addresses society's problems, and we're more interested in specialized graduate education that fits those narrow specialties than we are in teaching undergraduates. These perceptions are fueled by newspaper and television features that focus on how students in large research universities suffer through huge lecture sessions, how they find it increasingly difficult to register for courses they need to graduate (thus increasing the time and money they must invest in college), and how they rarely see senior professors, but are instead taught by graduate teaching assistants—often foreign—who don't speak English very well.

The question being asked with increasing regularity is, Just what do faculty members do? Studies of faculty workload have been commissioned in state after state, and together these studies indicate that college faculty members are working harder than ever—a remarkably consistent 55 hours per week from study to study—but they are probably teaching less, and they are almost certainly having less contact with students, particularly undergraduates. Needless to say, these findings do not sit well with our external constituencies. Neither do such stories as the one reported by Milton Greenberg (1993), whose university had just fired a full-time faculty member for holding down another full-time position at another university while receiving good evaluations for teaching, scholarship, and service at both places. As a university trustee asked when this case came to light, "What is the nature of faculty members' work, the structure of their days and weeks, that makes it possible for a faculty member to do that?" (p. A68).

Clearly, part of the problem lies in the nature of the discourse between the academy and its constituencies. The standard ways of describing our work to those outside of the academy, framed as they are in such statistics as instructional FTEs and grant money generated, simply do not describe very well the complex tasks facing modern faculty, and they are not very useful for assessing how effectively the modern university and its faculty contribute to the public good.

This volume has been written to explore how we might improve the public discourse about faculty work and to suggest how colleges and universities might document that work in a fashion that not only more faithfully describes what we do, but also results in reports that are more comprehensible and useful.

The first three chapters set the stage. In Chapter One, Margaret Miller describes the increasingly strident public concerns about higher education and analyzes how proposed governmental solutions are likely to affect how we define and measure faculty productivity. In Chapter Two, Steve Jordan reviews the findings and common elements from recent faculty workload studies and suggests a number of implications these studies have for higher education policy, particularly as the national focus shifts from the inputs of faculty effort to the outputs of student performance. In Chapter Three, Janet Lawrence provides a much-needed perspective for institutional researchers, namely how faculty members think about time. She shows how the academic culture makes faculty work difficult to partition accurately into "standardized temporal units." The inference is clear: if we are to arrive at a common discourse about faculty workload and productivity, we will have to examine assumptions about some basic terms, including the concept of time itself.

The next three chapters get down to practical issues, and lead off in Chapter Four with a case study written by Greer Glazer and Myron Henry of Kent State University. At Kent, the effort to better document faculty workload and productivity was part of a larger university effort to respond to new demands for restructuring and accountability within the State of Ohio; notable here is the comprehensive nature of Kent's workload study, which contained both quantitative and qualitative elements. There's enough detail given to allow for at least some transferability to other large complex institutions and to smaller campuses as well. In Chapter Five, Dennis Jones presents the outline of a new handbook for a national faculty data base, developed under the auspices of the National Center for Higher Education Management Systems (NCHEMS). Taking the position that faculty members are human assets and must be treated as such, the handbook seeks to establish a standard conceptual and definitional framework for faculty data, thus leading to greater comparability both within and across institutions. In Chapter Six, Lloyd Byrd builds on this framework and describes alternative methods to respond to increasingly complex institutional needs for information; he also provides some valuable practical tips that could come only from someone in the trenches.

The final chapter in the volume is by James Mingle and Richard Heydinger and returns to the more contextual flavor of the early chapters. Mingle and Heydinger are more speculative than analytical, however. They posit four external forces, already underway, as having the greatest potential for transforming faculty work in the next century. These are changes in government funding priorities, shifts in the global economy, pressures for increased privatization of government institutions (including, of course, colleges and universities), and the explosion of information technology.

Predictions of an impending social revolution and sober pronouncements about how higher education needs to reform itself are nothing new. What seems clear, not only from Mingle and Heydinger but also from the other contributors to this volume, is that our colleges and universities will no longer be able to maintain the insularity that has buffered these forces before. As faculty work changes, so must our documentation of it change—and the sooner we look to some of the alternatives described in this book, the better.

Jon F. Wergin
Editor

References

Greenberg, M. "Accounting for Faculty Members' Time." *Chronicle of Higher Education,* October 20, 1993, p. A68.
Zemsky, R. "An End to Sanctuary." *Policy Perspectives,* 1991, 3 (4), 1–7.

JON F. WERGIN is professor of educational studies at Virginia Commonwealth University in Richmond.

An analysis of the public pressures to measure and describe faculty work is presented, as well as a depiction of the forms those measures and descriptions are taking and how they are likely to evolve.

Pressures to Measure Faculty Work

Margaret A. Miller

In 1991, then-governor Wilder admonished Virginia's public college and university presidents that teaching must be their top priority. In the spring of 1992, after three straight years of cutting general-fund appropriations to higher education, the Virginia General Assembly directed the State Council of Higher Education to study the restructuring of higher education in the state. According to the 1992 Virginia Acts of Assembly, that restructuring was to include "revision of staffing guidelines to include minimum workload measures for faculty adjusted for type of institution, program, and the recognition of research conducted by the faculty." Into this landscape, a series of newspaper articles on higher education dropped like a bomb in the fall of 1993. The five-part series, cooperatively written and published by five Virginia newspapers, was summarized at its beginning this way:

Sunday: Getting through college is a tough struggle these days. Students juggle books and jobs, live with relatives, borrow, drop out, and choose schools close to home trying to make it.

Monday: It's smoke and mirrors. Look at the budgets of schools around the state, talk to officials, and you'll find that talk about paring down and containing costs of higher education is a sham. Budgets and staffs continue to grow, with little evidence of restructuring or economizing by colleges.

Tuesday: Some Virginia professors spend less time in the classroom each week than most people spend in their office each day. Even as state aid has been sliced, professors continue to be cut loose from what was once the mission of American universities—teaching.

Wednesday: With Virginia schools collecting more than $100 million a year from private sources to make up for fewer state dollars, some critics wonder what all that money is buying and what donors expect in return.

NEW DIRECTIONS FOR INSTITUTIONAL RESEARCH, no. 83, Fall 1994 © Jossey-Bass Publishers

Thursday: A lack of leadership at the state level has left colleges foundering as they try to adjust to booming enrollments and calls for more budget cuts. Also, some tips on filling out complicated financial aid forms and finding money to pay for college. ["Spiraling School Costs," p. A1]

The fact that concerns about higher education's structure and cost have been articulated by Virginia's legislators, governor, and press signals their depth and seriousness. Virginia is offered here as an illustration of a national phenomenon. The same concerns have led to faculty workload studies in Arizona, Colorado, Wisconsin, Hawaii, Ohio, Maryland, Florida, Mississippi, and South Carolina; in the last three states, faculty workloads have actually been mandated. The purpose of this chapter is to describe the nature and causes of the unprecedented level of public interest in how faculty members spend their time, as well as to suggest how the higher education community might respond to that interest.

Public Concerns About Higher Education

The central resentment that surfaced in the articles regarded the cost of tuition. In Virginia, a high-tuition state, general-fund cutbacks in the early 1990s had been more than compensated for by student revenues. Virginia students, who paid roughly a third of the cost of their education in 1989, pay almost half of it now, due to tuition increases of 45 percent. Anxiety over steeply rising tuition prompted the 1993 Virginia General Assembly, in House Joint Resolution number 142, to issue three separate study requests, one to look at the transitions between high school and college and between two- and four-year colleges, one to study the feasibility of a three-year degree, and a third to study barriers to graduation in four years. One of the a prior assumptions in the last study resolution began with the clause "Whereas the cost of a college education continues to escalate beyond the means of many middle-class families."

Problems of access to and affordability of public higher education are not unique to Virginia. During the 1990s, while tuition at private colleges across the country has risen at twice the rate of the Consumer Price Index, at public colleges it has risen at three times the rate (Gladieux, 1994). Even in a low-tuition state such as California, the California Higher Education Policy Center has identified the increasing difficulty of getting access to "the basic entry ticket to life in the American mainstream" as the central cause of public anxiety when it comes to higher education (Immerwahr, 1993, p. v). Alexander Astin's 1993 survey of first-year college students documents the same anxiety: A record one-third listed their college's tuition rate as an important reason for picking it, double the percentage who did so in 1976. Students are also more interested in financial aid. It is probably not a coincidence that record numbers of them listed their fathers as unemployed and their parents as divorced (Cage, 1994). Anxiety about tuition increases has spurred the development of prepaid tuition plans in a number of states, as well as proposals to limit tuition increases at public colleges and universities to the rate of inflation.

Hence the tone of the Virginia newspaper articles: the public sees higher education as the key to social mobility, and the promise of mobility is one of the most cherished articles of faith Americans have. No one wants to be stuck, or perhaps even worse, to see their children stuck, at a predetermined economic level. The American middle class, no less than its nineteenth-century British counterpart, can be described by Daniel Pool's sobriquet, "the upwardly anxious."

A college degree, though less and less a sufficient condition for economic and social advancement, is increasingly a necessary condition for it. As the *Postsecondary Education OPPORTUNITY* newsletter puts it, "Where educational attainment was once one of several means to a decent standard of living, the disappearance of the alternatives has left postsecondary education and training as the only means to that living standard" ("Economic Welfare," 1994, p. 13). Young people can no longer walk into the workplace with their high-school diplomas or their GEDs under their arms and expect to make a reasonable and secure living for themselves and their families. Because this is so, and because over the past several decades public colleges and universities have justified their expanded public support by promising an expanded range and number of students access to the middle class, higher education risks both consumer revolt and legislative intervention if it tries to solve its fiscal problems by closing its doors to students who have a reasonable chance of succeeding academically. California's enrollment cuts, for instance, were described as the "jackpot [higher education] issue" in the 1994 California legislative session (Thrombley, 1994, p. 1).

Causes of the Decline in Public Support

The decrease in general-fund support of higher education in Virginia, as in many other states, has two chief causes: an increase in competing demands—especially Medicaid, primary and secondary education, and prisons—and sluggish state revenues that are likely to remain so. One way to reverse the decline in higher education's funding would be to hold steady or increase its portion of the budget. Because public school enrollments are on the rise, however, school-funding formulas will drive up the costs of precollegiate education. Meanwhile, health care costs continue their seemingly inexorable (if slowed) climb and the immense popularity of state and national "three strikes and you're out" proposals suggests that the public's fear for its safety is likely to take precedence over longer-term social goods.

Tax hikes could increase total state revenues, but they have proven a serious political liability for those proposing them. In a recent newspaper article, reporters asked several Virginia legislators whether they were prepared to raise taxes to pay for higher education; their response was generally that they would consider doing so only if they were convinced that higher education had done all it could to control costs. The argument of the newspaper articles cited above is similar. College students are struggling hard to pay for their education, but before the taxpayers come to their relief, colleges and universities should do what they can to economize.

Although higher education can and does make the case that it has gotten more productive over the past years—by 1992, Virginia was serving 27 percent more students with 9 percent more staff than in 1980—it cannot or has not made a convincing case that it has controlled costs as much as possible. The public and legislators are full of common-sense suggestions about what more it might do. The American Association of University Professors reports that "at least 23 states have turned their attention, at some level or another, to the idea of closer supervision of higher education" ("The Work of Faculty. . ." 1994, p. 13). Because faculty salaries consume most of college budgets—often up to 80 percent—prominent among the suggestions are those designed to increase faculty productivity.

The Public's Solution

Studies of how many hours professors work generally indicate more than 50 hours a week (see Jordan's chapter in this volume). Most critics publicly concede that professors work hard, although they may privately express skepticism about the self-reported nature of the numbers. They do question how professors apportion their time, however. The Virginia newspaper articles argue that education costs more than it should because college professors do not teach enough. The "whereas" clauses attached to the 1992 Virginia General Assembly study resolution on barriers to graduation reflect similar assumptions. One of them was "Whereas ineffective counseling and lack of course planning can lead to changing majors and enrollment in an inadequate number of credit hours per semester." The bill's patron assumed that faculty do not spend enough time advising students or do it well when they do. Another "whereas" mentioned the nonavailability of classes as a reason for students' inability to finish their college degrees in four years. Clearly, some legislators think that faculty should spend more time teaching the classes students need to graduate.

As the employers of faculty, the public is not sure that their employees are engaged in the work that most needs to be done. The public is apt to believe that colleges and universities could effect great savings if they adjusted faculty work assignments to reflect what the public thinks faculty ought to be doing, rather than what the faculty thinks it ought to be doing. As one Virginia legislative staff member put it in a letter to the State Council of Higher Education's director: "You mentioned that the populi are suspicious and probably jealous of our institutions and our faculty. I agree. I think that the basis for that is the fact that higher education sets its own standards without involving common folk or even caring what common folk may think. My grandmother had no part in defining a 'first-rate' institution as one that expects less teaching from superstars" (Seaman, 1990). Although this suspicion taps a deeper, historic strain of anti-intellectualism in American society described by Richard Hofstadter in his book *Anti-Intellectualism in American Life* (1963), much of it is due to a gradual drifting apart of institutional culture from public need. Even the greater part of the public that is not hostile to higher education is increasingly reluctant to treat it as an unexamined good.

Faculty Reactions

College faculty are generally surprised and disheartened by the public outcry over their work lives. Conversations between Virginia's State Council of Higher Education staff and faculty throughout the commonwealth reveal that faculty feel unfairly singled out for scrutiny. Those at institutions focusing on teaching think that the press misrepresents their work; those at research institutions think that the public misunderstands the value of research and what they believe to be the positive relationship between scholarly work and teaching. They are startled by the edge of resentment that characterizes public criticisms of them.

Faculty surprise is not surprising. Many faculty members believe that they entered the profession under vows of poverty; in exchange, they expected to be exempted from the economic fluctuations of the larger society. The public does not see professors as underpaid, however, and the facts support its perception: although higher education supports comparatively few megasalaries, in 1992–1993 faculty income averaged about 17 percent higher than that of comparable professionals, such as engineers, scientists, teachers, and lawyers (Bureau of Labor Statistics, 1994, p. 243). Another fact also fuels public resentment: as professors have risen in the ranks of the middle class, that class has undergone a profound dislocation. To the recently unemployed white-collar worker, professorial salaries, the security of tenure, and the professor's control of his or her time all seem enviable. Other members of the middle class who are lucky enough to be employed are having to restructure their work and work harder; they are likely to be intolerant of those who consider it their right to be exempt from such necessities.

Many members of the academy share the public's worry that higher education may have become a self-enclosed and self-replicating institution that pays too little attention to the needs of the larger society. Despite pride in the research productivity of American universities since World War II, over the past decade many faculty, administrators, and educational leaders have become increasingly uneasy about the faculty reward system's increasing focus on research rather than on students. Donald Kennedy is not the only college president today who asserts that "it is time for us to reaffirm that education—that is, teaching in all its forms—is the primary task and that our society will judge us in the long run on how well we do it" (1990–1991, p. 9).

Research Under the Microscope

The academy must reexamine its emphasis on research for another reason as well: at its present rate of growth, that research has become unsustainable for its funders, producers, and consumers. Funders of research include the federal government, the states, and students, all of whom are taking a fresh look at their investments in this area. At the federal level, the end of the Cold War, the mounting deficit, competing demands for tax dollars, and generally diminished national economic competitiveness all have led to slowed increases in research funding. It was in this context that the House Committee on Science, Space, and Technology's Subcommittee on Science undertook a comprehensive review of U.S. research. Noting the way the faculty reward system puts increasingly competitive demands on that funding, the subcommittee's chair representative Rick Boucher said, "I worry about an academic research system with resources spread too thinly, with administrators and professors ever-more obsessed by fund raising, with a faltering educational vision and a waning sense of service to society. . . . Universities should reemphasize teaching in all its aspects, both inside and outside the classroom. In doing so, many institutions will have to curtail some of their research activities" (Boucher, 1993, p. B2).

States pay for research indirectly through professorial time allocated to departmental research. Because of that hidden subsidy, professorial teaching assignments are lighter in the research universities than they are in the community colleges. In Virginia, four years of budget reductions led state officials to calculate the salary costs of the proportion of time faculty reported spending on nonsponsored research and service combined. The total was roughly $200 million a year.

Finally, students foot the bill in the form of tuition increases that help pay professional salaries, which is one reason why private universities such as Syracuse and Stanford have joined the call for a rededication to teaching. Not only do private universities have to compete for the shrinking pool of students who can afford the tuition; they also need to cap tuition increases, which they can do only by making faculty salaries pay off in terms of increased teaching.

Meanwhile, some faculty are finding research demands increasingly onerous. The Carnegie Foundation's 1989 faculty survey, for instance, reveals faculty dissatisfaction with a reward system that weighs published and funded research more heavily than effective teaching. Many faculty members argue for the inescapable connection between teaching and research, but respected researchers, from Catherine Stimpson and William Schaefer in the humanities to Philip Abelson in science, complain about the triviality or specialization of much research and its decreasing relevance to undergraduate instruction (Mooney, 1991a; Abelson, 1993). Claims that teaching and research are synergistic must be balanced against the obvious ways in which they compete for a scholar's time. A University of California at Los Angeles survey revealed that "27 percent of all professors—and 44 percent of those at public universities—felt that demands for research interfered with teaching" (Mooney, 1991c, p. A16). Those who choose to spend their time on teaching find that the choice does not pay: in all types of institutions (including liberal arts colleges), teaching productivity is either not rewarded or is inversely proportional to salary (Fairweather, 1993).

Finally, the consumers of research are finding that the amounts produced are overloading their digestive capacities. Libraries are reeling under the escalating costs of an exponentially increasing volume of books and periodicals they have no space to store: the Modern Language Association's directory of periodicals contains about 3,200 journals and series in its domain alone (Mooney, 1991b). Consequently, libraries are turning to cooperative arrangements, from complementary collections-development plans supported by interlibrary loan to more modern forms of information-sharing. The 1994 Virginia General Assembly, for instance, funded the virtual library, an electronic database that will be accessible by all the public college and university libraries in the state. However, these strategies will not prevent libraries from canceling subscriptions to periodicals and refusing to buy books that receive little use. At the same time, many scholars, despairing of reading all relevant materials in their field, find themselves carving out an increasingly narrow portion of it in which to remain current or neglecting any research that is more than a few years old.

Workload Studies

Over the past few years, a number of attempts have been made to measure faculty workload, as analyzed in Chapter Two of this volume. Some are institutional, such as the one at Kent State University described in Chapter Four of this volume. Some associations, such as the American Association of University Professors (using data supplied by the U.S. Department of Education) or the State Higher Education Executive Officers organization, as well as some states have also conducted studies. In 1990, for instance, the State Council of Higher Education did such a study in Virginia. These studies, though remarkably consistent in reporting that faculty work somewhere between 47 and 57 hours per week, suffer from two major credibility problems.

The first is that they are generally based on faculty self-reporting. Because faculty members answer only to themselves about most of their time, there is no clearly feasible alternative to self-reports if researchers want to know how faculty spend their time; yet for the same reason, the public is apt to discount such assessments. The second problem is that many categories most central to the scholarly life, such as keeping up with the field and preparing courses, not to mention contemplation, are suspect to the public and clearly subject to ambiguity and even reporting abuse. The literature professor reading mystery novels or a public-policy professor watching a nightly newscast may be engaged in scholarship or preparation for teaching, but most people watching them would be hard-pressed to identify it as such. What professor sitting in the yard reading on a weekday morning has not wanted to tell an inquisitive neighbor, "Look! It's Plato! And in Greek!"? Finally, as Janet Lawrence points out in Chapter Three, given how faculty think about time, their work is extremely hard to categorize. For that reason, an approach where attention shifts from input to output or outcome criteria may be a more fruitful and publicly credible way to talk about faculty work.

Talk about it we must. C. S. Lewis, writing about the Protestant Reformation, says that the theological controversies of the time "could have been fruitfully debated only between mature and saintly disputants and at boundless leisure" but the debate was not possible because the participants "attracted fatal attention both of government and the mob" (1954, p. 37). His language is echoed 40 years later by that of Russell Edgerton, who says about the central controversies of the modern university, "Anyone who thinks that the academy has time for leisurely debate of these issues should spend an hour . . . reviewing the cascade of bills recently introduced in state legislatures around the country: bills to investigate faculty workload; bills to require institutional reports on a raft of items from student performance to the percentage of classes taught by TAs, adjunct faculty, and part-time faculty" (1993, p. 4).

The future holds in store no abatement of "government and mob" interest in this issue; the causes of that interest seem likely to persist. In many states, the discussion has already broadened, putting faculty productivity into a larger context. As Edgerton notes, indicators of institutional effectiveness, under development or in place in many states, are the newest manifestation of public concern with accountability. Attempts to quantify faculty productivity internal to the academy have always been crude, incomplete, or indirect: research funding levels, numbers of publications, or citation rates are simplistic, even as measures of scholarship. State-level reports on numbers of courses taught or hours spent in the classroom per week are more imperfect still as measures of the faculty's effect on students. If members of the higher education community do not develop credible and sophisticated alternatives, however, the public and its representatives will apply their common-sense definitions and categories to the academy, and the fit is often a bad one. There is also an overwhelming internal reason to describe better, and if necessary adjust, how faculty spend their time: if institutions do not find ways to extend the reach of their faculty, the hemorrhage of resources will leave them increasingly anemic.

Later chapters in this volume discuss both the difficulty of this task and some possible approaches to it. Past experience should suggest some criteria by which to evaluate our efforts. First, whatever studies we undertake should be rigorous and not self-serving; they should have the capacity to discriminate between the productive and the unproductive rather than to explain away public concerns. Second, studies should be designed to help those not initiated into the academic mysteries understand the complexities of professorial life and the many ways in which a faculty member can combine the elements of professorial responsibility. In order to meet these criteria of rigor and clarity, workload analysis should move beyond the individual to the unit, probably to the department or program. These analysis must combine hard data with explanatory narrative that is comprehensible to the college-educated nonacademic.

Finally, if we do not want faculty work to be paid by the hour, productivity studies should focus on the outcomes of faculty work: tangible evidence of student learning, research, and public service. Public and private colleges and universities ultimately will be judged, and their level of support determined, not by how hard faculty work or even what they work at, but by the caliber and success of their graduates and by the institutions' contributions to their communities and to society.

References

Abelson, P. H. "The American Research University." *Science,* 1993, *262,* 487.

Boucher, R. "A Science Policy for the 21st Century." *Chronicle of Higher Education,* September 1, 1993, p. B2.

Bureau of Labor Statistics of the U.S. Department of Labor. *Employment and Earnings,* 1994, *41* (1).

Cage, M. C. "Beyond the B.A." *Chronicle of Higher Education,* January 26, 1994, p. A29.

"Economic Welfare and Educational Attainment." *Postsecondary Education OPPORTUNITY,* 1994, *19,* 13.

Edgerton, R. "The Tasks Faculty Perform." *Change,* July–Aug. 1993, p. 4.

Fairweather, J. S. "Faculty Reward Structures: Toward Institutional Homogenization." *Research in Higher Education,* 1993, *34* (5), 603–623.

Gladieux, L. E. "The Tuition Spiral." *CrossTalk,* 1994, *2* (1), 10.

Hofstadter, R. *Anti-Intellectualism in American Life.* New York: Knopf, 1963.

Immerwahr, J., and Farkas, S. *The Closing Gateway: Californians Consider Their Higher Education System.* San Jose: The Public Agenda Foundation for the California Higher Education Policy Center, September 1993.

Kennedy, D. "Planning for Stanford's Next Twenty Years." *Planning for Higher Education,* 1990–1991, *19,* 6.

Lewis, C. S. *English Literature in the 16th Century, Excluding Drama.* Oxford: Clarendon Press, 1954.

Mooney, C. J. "Efforts to Cut Amount of 'Trivial' Scholarship Win New Backing from Many Academics." *Chronicle of Higher Education,* May 22, 1991a, pp. A13, 16.

Mooney, C. J. "In 2 Years, a Million Refereed Articles, 300,000 Books, Chapters, Monographs." *Chronicle of Higher Education,* May 22, 1991b, p. A17.

Mooney, C. J. "Professors Feel Conflict Between Roles in Teaching and Research, Say Students Are Badly Prepared." *Chronicle of Higher Education,* May 8, 1991c, pp. A15–A16.

Seaman, R. Unpublished letter to Gordon K. Davies, December 20, 1990.

"Spiraling School Costs Force Some to Defer Their Dream." *Richmond Times-Dispatch,* September 12, 1993, p. A1.

Thrombley, W. "'Downsizing': CSU Trims Enrollment to Match State Support." *CrossTalk,* 1994, *2* (1), 1

"The Work of Faculty: Expectations, Priorities, and Rewards." Washington, D.C.: The American Association of University Professors, 1994.

MARGARET A. MILLER is associate director for academic and student affairs at the State Council of Higher Education for Virginia.

The findings and methodologies from recent faculty workload studies are reviewed and implications for higher education policy are suggested.

What We Have Learned About Faculty Workload: The Best Evidence

Stephen M. Jordan

How do faculty spend their time? Faculty workload studies attempt to answer this question about the single largest allocation of resources, both human and fiscal, in our colleges and universities. In more complex terms, however, faculty workload studies are undertaken in order to understand faculty resources and to manipulate how they are deployed. Consequently, once the initial question about faculty workload is asked and institutions begin to answer the inquiry, the simplicity is lost and complexity takes over. The process of answering the question becomes not only technically complex, but laden with perceptions by both the inquirer and the focus of the question, the faculty.

Is the initial question fair? Absolutely. Is it in the interest of colleges and universities to study faculty workload? Without a doubt, because failure to address and understand the distribution of faculty effort has policy dimensions for each institution that will affect its ability to achieve its role and mission. However, the evidence suggests that faculty workload studies are no more than a means to a more important end: improvement in learning.

There are widespread concerns that faculty value research more than teaching. The evidence offered to support this perception is the undisputed fact that many faculty spend only six to ten hours per week in the classroom. As one author has noted (Layzell, 1992), many public policy makers believe that faculty care little about undergraduate education, particularly at the lower division, and are more concerned with their graduate students, research, publication, and other professional activities. Classroom contact (teaching load) studies are certainly one measure of faculty effort. As Dennis Jones and Lloyd Byrd note later in this volume, however, such studies capture only a portion of the faculty effort toward instruction. Workload studies are an attempt to display the breadth and depth of the entire faculty effort and to relate it to the roles and missions of institutions.

I have two objectives in this chapter. First, I will review the findings and summarize the common elements from recent faculty workload studies. Second, I will comment on the implications faculty workload studies have for higher education policy, particularly the shifting national focus from the inputs of faculty effort to the outputs of student performance.

Recent Workload Studies

In response to widespread perceptions that faculty spend too little time teaching and too much time participating in research or consulting, some states have turned to faculty workload studies to determine how faculty spend their time. A recent national study (see Table 2.1) corroborated the widely shared belief among faculty that faculty devote a considerable amount of time to their work, between fifty-two and fifty-seven hours per week. Other studies have had similar findings (Blackburn and Lawrence, 1988; Serpe, Newton, and Vandewater, 1990; State Council of Higher Education for Virginia, 1991; Arizona Joint Legislative Budget Committee, 1993). Furthermore, these studies clearly demonstrate that the distribution of faculty effort among the traditional elements of instruction, research, and service is affected by the role and mission of the institution. That is, in each study, faculty in research universities spent less time on instruction and more time on research than did faculty in doctoral or comprehensive universities (see Table 2.2). The inverse is obviously true for faculty at comprehensive and doctoral universities, with faculty spending more time on instruction and less time on research than did their colleagues in research universities. The proportion of time spent on administrative activities is generally consistent across all types of institutions.

Methodologies. Two predominant methodologies have been used in recent studies of faculty workload. The first is activity reporting. A work period is specified (one day or one week, for example) and faculty report the amount of time they spend on each of the activities for which there is a standard definition in the report. Activity reporting was the methodology used in the previously cited studies. These types of studies attempt to answer two questions: How much time do faculty work? and How do faculty allocate their time? Interestingly, although workload studies that use activity reporting have received widespread attention, very few have been conducted on a statewide basis.

The second methodology is the equivalency report. In this method, faculty relate their activity to a credit-hour standard for the institution. Each faculty activity is converted to the standard. For example, teaching a credit hour course is equivalent to at least three credit hours, but may be worth more if the class is large. Supervising an independent student is equivalent to a fraction of the credit earned by the student. The sum of each faculty member's credits should be at least equal to the institutional standard.

Table 2.1. Faculty Workload: Full-Time Faculty at Public Institutions, Fall 1987

Type of Institution	Average Hours Worked Per Week
Public research	57
Public doctoral	55
Public comprehensive	52
All institutions (public and private)	53

Source: National Center for Education Statistics, 1991.

Table 2.2. Percent of Faculty Effort Allocated to Activities

Type of Institution	Teaching	Research	Administration	All Other
Public research	43	29	14	16
Public doctoral	47	22	14	17
Public comprehensive	62	11	13	13
All institutions (public and private)	56	16	13	16

Source: National Center for Education Statistics, 1991.

Common Elements in Activity Reporting. Faculty workload studies based on activity reporting with an identified work period have received the most attention because they typically share several elements in common. The most basic of these elements is the quantification of faculty workload within the traditional tripartite mission of instruction, research, and service. These three general categories of faculty effort form the common thread that permits some statistical comparison to be made among the various workload studies. However, the discrete definitions that make up each major category often vary among the studies. For example, within the category of instruction, classroom contact will most likely include direct instructional contact with both undergraduate and graduate students in a regularly scheduled class, lab, workshop, ensemble, or production, but it may not include individualized instruction. Clinical patient care and student-directed activity are also likely to be accounted for in different ways. Class preparation, grading, office hours, and advising may be categorized as instruction in recognition of the fact that they may occur simultaneously or overlap. Within the category of research, separation of externally sponsored research, state-funded organized research, departmentally or institutionally funded research, and other research or creative activity including creation of works in the visual arts or music is often not consistently defined.

The consequence of definitional differences is that only limited analysis primarily related to mission and comparisons of workload can be made among the various workload studies. However, these cross-study limitations do not necessarily defeat the policy purposes for which workload studies may be used, nor do they negate the ability of individual states, systems, or institutions to have a consistent analysis of the distribution of faculty effort, as long as they are careful to define the workload activities consistently.

The second common element of faculty workload studies is an analysis based on a typical faculty work week. There are two principal reasons for choosing a work week as the preferred measurement. First, it is long enough to capture all of the activities a faculty member might engage in during a finite period of time. Second, most people can relate to the concept of a work week, so for the purposes of public policy and informing individuals not normally associated with higher education, it is an acceptable, if not preferred, measurement.

The third common element is the use of self-reported data through surveys. Most states, and indeed most institutions, do not have ongoing faculty time and effort reports; faculty workload studies typically have to create a data set. Consequently, faculty workload studies are subject to all of the methodological concerns associated with survey work, including survey method and follow-up, whether to survey all faculty or a sample, and issues of individual faculty member confidentiality, to name just a few. Analysis at the departmental level may be limited due to small sample sizes and care must be taken not to draw conclusions on data that are not statistically significant. Finally, critics of self-report studies suggest that the use of self-reported data leads to inflated workload results. Supporters of self-reported data believe that consistency of responses over long periods of time lends validity to the typical findings that faculty work fifty-two to fifty-seven hours per week.

Analytical Concerns. As noted previously, the genesis of faculty workload studies is the widely held belief that faculty spend too much time doing research and too little time in the classroom. This belief is so strongly held by some that it can lead to biased analysis.

The strength of a faculty workload study lies in its ability to convey the entirety of the faculty effort. It does this by mirroring the tripartite mission of instruction, research, and public service and by displaying faculty effort in each of these important categories. As noted earlier, most studies collect information based on definitions or subcategories of each major category and then sum the information to the categories of instruction, research, and service for comparison with other studies and for simplification of analysis and reporting.

Sometimes staff members to state policy makers disaggregate instructional activity into its subcomponents (direct classroom instruction, direct individual instruction, clinical activity, and classroom preparation) and compare each against the total for another category, such as research. This procedure is particularly common if staff are unfamiliar with the way faculty accomplish their work and with the joint products associated with much of the faculty's efforts.

The implications are obvious. For example, if faculty spend 47 percent of their time on instruction, of which 14 percent is direct classroom instruction, and the direct classroom instruction is compared with the 33 percent of total time spent on research, state policy makers might conclude that faculty do not care about teaching.

Another analytical concern is the potential for researchers to draw conclusions on the basis of comparisons of simple averages rather than conducting tests of significance. Conclusions in workload studies can imply a significance or certainty that cannot be supported by the survey data. Tests of significance must be conducted to determine whether the groups being compared are actually different, particularly when the size of a group or the difference between groups is small.

Policy Implications

Recent faculty workload studies have had a profound effect on higher education. Most observers would acknowledge that faculty workload studies have been initiated for one purpose, namely to increase teaching productivity, either through increased class size, more scheduled courses per faculty member, or increased total workload. Judged against those objectives, faculty workload studies have been a failure. Judged against other objectives, however, they have been a success.

Reevaluating the Value of Teaching. It is difficult to believe that there can be any further improvement in the productivity of faculty as measured by hours worked in a week. Clearly, fifty-two to fifty-seven hours per week is a major commitment by faculty to their jobs. Many observers of higher education have noted that faculty are working harder than ever before. This view is corroborated by earlier studies that showed average work weeks ranging from forty-two to forty-six hours per week, approximately ten hours per week less than studies conducted only eleven years later. However, even though total workload has risen, many observers believe that instructional loads, particularly at the more prestigious research universities, have declined to embarrassingly low levels.

A changing faculty workload has significant implications for the quality of the undergraduate experience. Several of the faculty workload studies found that when asked how faculty would like to allocate their time, faculty responded that they would like to reduce the amount of time spent on class preparation and advising and increase the amount of time spent on research. Contrast these findings with those of Pascarella and Terenzini (1991), who suggest that individualized and small-group interactions between students and faculty outside of the classroom have significant positive effects on a wide variety of educational outcomes. One would expect that the opportunity for those kinds of interactions would be greatest in institutions where faculty spend more time on instruction and in preparation and advising.

Despite this trend, a number of surveys show that faculty believe that teaching is very important. Buoyed by these findings, some universities are engaging in a redefinition of teaching that incorporates classroom performance, assessment of student work, supervision of graduate students, and course preparation and advising. Clearly, there is a trend toward a more inclusive definition of teaching.

Enhancing Student Productivity. There is little or no documented evidence that faculty workload studies have resulted in a change in the distribution of an institution's total faculty effort. There are however, indications that faculty workload studies are contributing to a shift in focus from the inputs of faculty effort to the outputs of enhancing learning and educational quality. For example, one state that completed a faculty workload study opted not to implement teaching or workload requirements, but rather adopted the following set of objectives to link faculty teaching effort to the improvement of the quality of undergraduate education (Arizona Joint Legislative Budget Committee, 1993):

Students will be able to register for the classes necessary for meeting their general education and major requirements when they need them.

Students will receive adequate advising for their program and career needs.

Classrooms will be adequately equipped for instruction, using modern instructional technology.

The number of lower-division courses taught by ranked faculty will be increased.

Graduates will be properly trained and educated to compete in their chosen fields.

There will be an increase in student contact with ranked faculty in the many aspects of the students' educational experience.

Undergraduates will be more completely integrated into research-related activities.

These objectives coincide with one senior higher education executive's observation that higher education must focus more on student learning and less on faculty productivity (Johnstone, 1993). Student productivity enhancement is viewed as more substantial and sustainable than increasing faculty workload to affect student outcomes.

Providing further evidence of the shift in emphasis away from workload enhancement and toward student productivity is a recent report (Russell, 1992) that found that only a quarter of the respondents cited faculty workload and productivity as an important state issue and priority, whereas undergraduate education and effectiveness and accountability in higher education were both identified by half the respondents as important state issues.

Role and Mission. On a statewide basis, faculty workload studies have had the positive effect of reinforcing the importance of role and mission. There is not much doubt that many higher education institutions participated in mission drift between 1975 and 1990. One study documented this drift (State Council of Higher Education for Virginia, 1991), finding that faculty at both doctoral and comprehensive universities increased the proportion of time spent on research while decreasing the proportion of time spent on service. The study also documented that faculty at doctoral institutions had decreased time spent on instructional activities.

As a consequence of the recent faculty workload studies, state policy makers appear to have a renewed interest in wanting to make conscious decisions about the balance between research and teaching in research universities, as contrasted with other institutions whose missions place greater emphasis on teaching. This is not to suggest that all institutions should have the same distribution of effort across the various workload categories. It does suggest, however, that each state should ensure that faculty effort is going toward teaching, research, and public service in a balance that meets state needs, not simply institutional aspirations (Jordan and Layzell, 1992).

Indeed, at least one state (Arizona Joint Legislative Budget Committee, 1993) is using its faculty workload study to help it plan for enrollment growth. State higher education officials have examined the implications of starting new campuses, using the research institutions' standard instructional load of five courses per year; they then evaluated the effects of adding one additional course and three additional courses per faculty member. The results are startling. If one course is added to the workload, the number of tenure-track faculty required for a campus of 10,000 FTE students is reduced by 72 FTE faculty, a savings of $4.5 million. If the course load is increased to eight courses per year, an increase of three courses per faculty member, the tenure-track faculty requirements are reduced by 162 FTE faculty, a savings of $10.1 million per year. This state is planning for three campuses of 10,000 FTE students each.

Other Workload Models. Perhaps as important as changing the total distribution of faculty effort within an institution, faculty workload studies play an important role in examining the individual contributions that faculty make to the instruction, research, and service priorities of departments and colleges. They provide an opportunity to examine how faculty within an academic unit accomplish the collective responsibilities of the unit; in so doing, they raise fundamental questions concerning how faculty accomplish their work. For example, is the individual fulfillment of the tripartite mission of instruction, research, and service still a valid model? Or should alternatives be examined that better recognize that individuals do not necessarily contribute equally to teaching, research, and service? By considering faculty workload in total, academic units can begin recognizing and planning for differences in faculty development needs and can better determine how individual faculty members might better contribute in any given year toward the academic unit's mission.

Faculty workload studies have also contributed to more frank discussions about faculty reward systems, particularly rewards for teaching and how they relate to the achievement of an academic unit's mission. The evidence seems clear that the reward structure benefits those who have strong credentials in peer-reviewed research, regardless of that faculty member's contribution to the other facets of the academic unit's mission. The rewards take several forms, including higher salaries, better laboratory space and equipment, and more support by graduate research assistants. The debate about faculty workload and the stated desire of public policy makers to place greater focus on teaching and the quality of the educational experience has encouraged faculty to question the reward systems and to demand changes if policy makers truly want faculty to spend more time on instruction. Governing boards and institutional executives are now stating their agreement and intent that faculty should establish an annual work plan with their departmental chair in which they agree on the faculty member's stated contributions for the next year to instruction, research, and service and then provide merit salary increases to reflect fulfillment of that work plan.

Conclusion

Faculty workload studies are a response to perceptions that faculty spend too little time in the classroom and too much time conducting research. The results of faculty workload studies have to some extent moderated these perceptions because the studies have consistently shown that faculty work hard, fifty-two to fifty-seven hours per week, and they spend the greatest proportion of their time, approximately 50 percent, on instruction-related activities.

Although faculty workload studies have not resulted in demonstrable changes in the allocation of faculty effort, they have helped contribute to a change in the focus of higher education accountability from the inputs of faculty effort to the outputs of enhanced learning and educational quality. It is in this arena, enhancing learning and quality, that many believe the greatest productivity improvements can be made. If this is true, does it also mean that interest in faculty workload studies will wane and eventually die out? Probably not. Faculty workload studies seem to have a cycle that closely mirrors the capacity of states to fund ongoing operations. As state resources tighten and competition among competing programs becomes greater, interest in faculty productivity increases.

More importantly though, interest in enhancing student productivity, like faculty workload studies themselves, has yet to provide empirical evidence of a change in outcome. The empirical evidence in faculty workload studies would be a demonstrated shift in the allocation of time from one category of effort to another. Though difficult to accomplish, such a shift is at least verifiable. The empirical evidence in student productivity would be a demonstrated change in mastery by students of curricular content and improvement in technological capacities. Here, little agreement exists even on how to measure or demonstrate a change in student outcomes. Absent consensus measures, there will always be a tendency to fall back on examining the method of production, which means continued examinations of faculty workload in the future.

References

Arizona Joint Legislative Budget Committee, Higher Education Research Section. *Arizona Faculty Workload Study: Findings and Policy Issues.* Phoenix: Joint Legislative Budget Committee, 1993.

Blackburn, R., and Lawrence, J. *Faculty at Work.* Ann Arbor: National Center for Research to Improve Postsecondary Teaching and Learning, University of Michigan, 1988.

Johnstone, D. B. *Learning Productivity: A New Imperative for American Higher Education.* Albany: State University of New York, 1993.

Jordan, S. M., and Layzell, D. T. *A Case Study of Faculty Workload Issues in Arizona: Implications for State Higher Education Policy.* Denver: State Higher Education Executive Officers, 1992.

Layzell, D. T. "Tight Budgets Demand Studies of Faculty Productivity." *Chronicle of Higher Education,* February 19, 1992, pp. B2–B3.

National Center for Education Statistics. *Profiles of Faculty in Higher Education Institutions, 1988.* Washington, D.C.: U.S. Department of Education, Office of Educational Research and Improvement, 1991.

Pascarella, E. T., and Terenzini, P. T. *How College Affects Students: Findings and Insights from Twenty Years of Research.* San Francisco: Jossey-Bass, 1991.

Russell, A. B. *Faculty Workload: State and System Perspectives.* Denver: State Higher Education Executive Officers, 1992.

Serpe, R. T., Newton, R. R., and Vandewater, S. R. *CSU Faculty Workload Study.* Fullerton: Social Science Research Center, California State University–Fullerton, 1990.

State Council of Higher Education for Virginia. *Results of the Virginia Faculty Survey.* Richmond: State Council of Higher Education for Virginia, 1991.

STEPHEN M. JORDAN *is executive director of the Kansas Board of Regents.*

The literature on organizational culture frames a discussion of time-related demands on faculty and explains why it is difficult to segment faculty work into standardized temporal units.

Campus Culture and Faculty Perceptions of Time

Janet H. Lawrence

A decade ago in the ASHE-ERIC Report on faculty workload, Henard (in Yuker, 1984) said, "The impression is widespread among legislators that faculty members have easy jobs involving working only a few hours a week, nine months of the year" (p. 5). Today the impression persists, and writers such as Heydinger and Simsek (1992, p. 1) portray the productivity of faculty as the issue that goes "to the heart of the concerns expressed by critics of higher education." Likewise, faculty responses to such criticism have not changed. As was the case in the 1980s, faculty continue to respond with cynicism to such rebukes and to distrust studies of their work habits.

Imbedded in the discourse about faculty productivity are assumptions regarding the temporal aspects of faculty work as well as the links between the use of time by faculty, their productivity, and the effectiveness of colleges and universities. The temporal aspects of work include cultural and individual perspectives about time as well as the temporal patterning of work within an organization. The cultural perspective is the predominant way members think about, define, and arrange time in their lives. An individual's perspective is the way he or she experiences time: whether it passes quickly, whether the individual is satisfied with the amount of time he or she can allocate to an activity, and so forth. The temporal patterning of work is the sequencing of activities that emerges as people use the time available to them: the regularizing of certain activities, timing activities to correspond with periods of phases in cycles, and so on.

In this chapter, I use the literature on organizational culture to frame a discussion of the time-related demands on faculty and to explain why it is difficult to segment faculty work into standardized temporal units. I also use the literature on how time is experienced to explain why faculty distrust estimates of their workload made by independent observers.

Temporal Aspects of Organizational Culture

Schriber and Gutek (1987) note that there are very few studies of how time is experienced and used within organizations. However, they state, "Time is a basic dimension of organizations. How time is partitioned, scheduled and used has both dramatic and subtle influences on organizations and the people in them. For organizations, the effective scheduling, coordination, and synchronization of people and tasks through time is a key to survival, growth, and profitability. For employees, the effective scheduling and use of time across tasks both at work and outside work can affect their performance and satisfaction, on the job and off" (p. 642).

Higher education researchers recognize that college and university faculty are members of multiple cultures, each having its own set of normative expectations for their behavior and productivity (Light, 1974; Parsons and Platt, 1973; Clark, 1989; Tierney, 1991). They are members of a particular college or university, a department, an area of specialization, and other collegial groups; each is also part of at least one discipline group (some faculty in professional schools belong to a root discipline as well as a field of practice; biochemistry is a root discipline of medicine, for example). However, little or nothing has been published about how time is experienced and used in these organizational cultures and the implications for faculty job performance and satisfaction. What kinds of pressure are created by the time-related normative expectations that predominate and to what extent do they foster or hinder faculty productivity?

In the next section, I consider the time perspectives evident within campus and discipline cultures and speculate on how different orientations to time are manifest in the norms for faculty and in their work patterns. The perspectives of time are not always consistent; even when they are, segmenting and sequencing activities for the purpose of defining workload can be problematic.

Cultural Time Perspectives and Temporal Features of Activity Patterns. Cultural orientations to time differ and are reflected in the norms that guide behavior within an organization (Schriber and Gutek, 1987). Graham (1981) has identified three general cultural perspectives of time based on a review of anthropological research. One orientation or model is called linear-separable. The key assumption is that time can be subdivided into discrete units and these units can be "quantified and compared easily with other quantifiable items, such as money or other resources" (Owen, 1991, p. 347). Time is characterized as objective, measurable, unidirectional, and infinitely divisible, and activities are regulated by clocks and calendars (Lauer, 1981; Schriber and Gutek, 1987). The second cultural model is called circular-traditional, where the relevant unit of time is a period or phase in a cycle when the time is right for certain activities, such as an agricultural season or human development stage. Calendar time is less relevant than the onset and end of the temporal units; cycles and seasons can vary from individual to individual or year to year. However, it is assumed that the future will resemble the past in that the same conditions will recur. The third orientation or model is called procedural-traditional. The focus here is on the activity being done and not on the time it takes to complete it or how it fits within a cycle. Time as measured by minutes or hours is unimportant. As is the case in rituals, for example, conducting the activity properly and carrying it to an appropriate conclusion are what matter (Owen, 1991).

Differences in cultural orientations are reflected in the temporal dimension of norms, the expectations about time that guide role performance, and the sanctions on the use of time that influence behavior. Ultimately, these pressures lead within a social group or organization to characteristic activity patterns that vary in periodicity, tempo, timing, and duration (Lauer, 1981; Lim and Seers, 1993).

Periodicity is the rhythm of life within an organization. It is fostered by organizational activities and by the needs of the members that occur regularly and can be mapped into time periods. For example, faculty meetings are an activity within academic departments that are regularized so that people know when there will be an opportunity to ask questions, raise concerns, and make decisions. Class periods are regulated by the clock and can be plotted out in a weekly schedule. Commenting on the rhythm of activities, students and faculty often describe their course schedule as good or bad depending on the distribution of class sessions. Individual factors that affect the rhythm include a person's social-psychological or physical readiness to engage in an activity. For instance, faculty members may try to allocate time to writing first thing in the morning if they find this is when they are most creative. Similarly, students might discover a best time in the day for them personally to study.

Tempo is the frequency with which activities occur within a measured time period. The pace of life is assumed to be fast if this period is filled with activity and slow if it is unfilled. Furthermore, tempo can vary in intensity. Some activities are of higher priority to an organization or hold greater personal meaning for individuals; more is at stake when they engage in the high-priority activities. Intensity is this level of engagement, and is exemplified by the tempo of academic life at the beginning of the academic year when many events occur that are of critical importance to the faculty and college, such as orientation, advising, and the beginning of class. Counting the hours in a work week simply fails to convey a sense of tempo.

Timing is the way in which different activities are coordinated. Within a time period, activities may be done simultaneously, as when a chemistry faculty member works in her lab on her own research and supervises her graduate students' projects. Other times, the activities must be done in sequence; for example, one phase of an experiment must be done before another can begin.

In the first instance, the timing of activities is synchronized but in the second, the timing of activities is coordinated, as they are linked in a linear fashion.

Finally, an activity can vary in terms of the amount of time required to complete it, or duration. In organizational cultures with a linear-separable orientation, emphasis is placed on precise measurement because time is a resource that must be managed, and efficient use of time is a key component of organizational effectiveness. It is assumed that organizations and the people within them have a great deal of control over the work environment and individuals are socialized to time by task expectations. However, from the circular-traditional and procedural-traditional perspectives, duration depends on many factors that may or may not be under one's control; the time to task completion can only be estimated based on past experiences (circular-traditional) or the duration is simply how long it takes to do the activity properly (procedural-traditional). To illustrate, gathering survey data depends on factors within faculty control (preparing the survey items) and factors outside of faculty control (the mail, printing, response of subjects).

What cultural time orientations predominate in colleges and universities? How are these orientations manifest in the norms that regulate faculty behavior and the periodicity, tempo, timing, and duration of their activities?

Campus Culture.   One cannot speak of a college campus as having a single cultural orientation to time. Within postsecondary institutions, all three time perspectives shape the norms for faculty. A linear-separable view of time guides the overall management of the institution and has especially strong effects on the instructional activities of a campus. Administrators subdivide and create temporal units for the various institutional activities based on their assumptions about time requirements such as the amount of class meeting time (number and length of class periods) that constitutes a semester-length course. The costs associated with these units guide budget decisions such as how much tuition to charge per credit hour or how much to pay an adjunct professor to teach a course. Calendar- and clock-regulated schedules and deadlines impose coherence and predictability on the various activities, an orderliness that reduces student, faculty, and staff feelings of uncertainty.

Circular- and procedural-traditional perspectives are also apparent in campus cultures. Many activities are carried out in a cyclic fashion, repeating year after year, term after term, symbolizing the beginning and end of a period or phase. For example, sabbaticals follow a seven-year cycle and the academic year or semester has recurring phases (matriculation, midterms, finals, convocation, graduation, reunions). Although these cycles are to varying degrees tied to a calendar year, they are also determined by a sense of timing derived from past experience; midterms, for example, do not necessarily meet a strict calendar definition but occur instead when the faculty member believes that students are ready for assessment or that the right amount of material has been presented.

The procedural-traditional view of time permeates norms regarding faculty scholarship: programs of scholarship, sustained inquiry efforts, progress in fits and starts, moving down blind alleys as well as productive avenues. Adding to the knowledge base of one's discipline or field is the goal and a professor is expected to persist until it is achieved. Scholarship is regulated not only by the tenure and promotion clock (circular-traditional) but by self-imposed deadlines and a sense of when a project is complete. (The next section deals with the culture of funding agencies as part of the discipline and discusses the time perspectives that predominate here).

The social constructions of time or accepted ways of marking the passage of time that follow from this combination of linear-separable, circular, and procedural-traditional time perspectives provide the framework for and contribute to the rhythm of faculty life. The question remains: To what extent are these orientations evident in the faculty norms and their teaching and research activity patterns?

Periodicity. Although the academic year is not synonymous with the calendar year, it always begins and ends in roughly the same months and there is comfort in this predictability. The academic year is a socially constructed unit of time that fulfills both the organization's need for order among its various activities and individuals' need for consistency. Faculty and students become comfortable with the rhythm of semesters or quarters, develop behavior patterns around it, and do not like disruptions. A linear-segmental orientation to time is evident in the student and teacher norms regarding course loads. Each has underlying assumptions about how much out-of-class time is required to prepare for a class.

A circular-traditional influence is also evident in learning and teaching norms and activity patterns for students and faculty. For example, new students are expected to go through a period of adjustment to college and orientation activities are created in response; faculty are expected to take this transitional phase into account in their teaching. Faculty become accustomed to preparing for and teaching courses in a particular pattern, and they structure their activities accordingly. What to outsiders may appear as tinkering with the schedule is not viewed as such by students and faculty because they have come to expect that courses and activities will repeat within a cycle; that is, teaching activities will predominate within certain periods and scholarship within others.

Scholarly norms certainly have some segmental-linear features (data must be gathered before they can be analyzed); however, activity patterns in this area are greatly affected by individual faculty needs and quality standards. Developing one's expertise tends to proceed in stages or cycles. The same activity can vary in the clock time required to do it as a result of glitches in data gathering, access to books, or other factors, and there are instances when one is simply not making progress and must break off from the activity and get back to it whenever the conditions are right. How much time one has to set aside for writing, for example, varies across individuals. Past experience tells faculty they need a certain amount of time to get their heads into their work, gather necessary resources, and make productive use of time set aside for this activity. In the sciences, there may be narrow windows of opportunity for an experiment that are determined by the reproductive cycle of a specimen.

Duration. Scholarship does not necessarily have clear beginning and end points; one is constantly reading, writing, editing, and revising. Reading in one area can lead to another, and another, in a never-ending process of becoming informed, checking sources, being on the cutting edge. Serendipitous findings in a laboratory experiment can send a researcher in new and unanticipated directions. Writing is complete when the faculty member believes he or she has done what is necessary and the manuscript is judged to be acceptable. Hence, the norms and patterns of activities that constitute scholarship tend to be organized around circular- and procedural-traditional views of time. The exception is sponsored research, projects funded by an outside agency. In this case, the faculty member's behavior is affected by a different set of norms, which are discussed in the next section on discipline culture.

Tempo. Faculty activity patterns within a semester or quarter vary in tempo, pace, and intensity. The tempo at the beginning and end of a semester is fast-paced and intense. Important teaching-related activities—advising, ordering books, grading, preparing for the next term, perhaps coordinating the work of TAs, and participating in graduation—all converge. Over the term, the pace and intensity of teaching and scholarship can vary depending on the organization's needs, such as deadlines for grades, new course proposals, student fellowships, and internal grant money, and depending on the meaningfulness or importance of the activities to the faculty member. Tempo also varies in response to individual student and faculty needs throughout the term—students asking for help around the time of exams or when papers are due, faculty imposing pressure on themselves to complete a task, and so forth.

Timing. Although faculty activities can be distinguished, it is difficult to segment the time spent on each one because they tend more often to be coincidental and synchronized than to be interdependent and coordinated. Departmental decisions that are prerequisite to decisions at the college level, such as admissions, financial aid, grading, faculty searches, and hiring, are coordinated faculty activities. The organization must coordinate the decision-making processes of different units and consequently, sequencing is invariant, and faculty have set deadlines. However, a large portion of faculty activities are apparently independent of one another. Faculty serve on committees and task forces within their colleges, work on several manuscripts simultaneously, supervise students' research, and teach courses. The activities are at best loosely related and do not necessarily lend themselves to linear ordering. As a result, faculty come to expect autonomy with respect to setting priorities and scheduling their work times, for this norm enables them to be productive in a setting that depends on the synchronization of activities.

In brief, there are many cultural orientations to time on college campuses that affect faculty teaching and scholarly norms and activity patterns. On some occasions, the relevant temporal unit is the calendar or clock time—for example, the faculty member has a certain amount of time to submit grades after the scheduled final exam for a course. Often, the relevant time unit is a phase of adjustment that varies in duration or time is irrelevant, there are no clock or calendar-linked prescriptions, and one keeps at tasks such as directing a student's dissertation or personal writing until it is finished. As in the procedural-traditional cultural view, measured time is unimportant and performing properly is paramount. Highlighting the temporal dimension of faculty norms enables one to see where segmenting their activities into monthly or annual production units may be appropriate and where it is inappropriate.

Culture of Disciplines. Faculty are members of organizations that extend beyond their campus boundaries: disciplinary and professional associations are a case in point. As happens on college campuses, the dominant views of time are infused into the norms that guide members' behavior. The predominant view most likely varies by discipline, but in most instances it tends to be circular and procedural-traditional.

The cyclicity of disciplinary cultures is manifest in such aspects as the timing of the annual research conferences, the award competitions within these associations, the honoring of promising scholars, and the journal publication schedules. A more subtle manifestation is represented by disciplinary norms in some domains regarding how much time can elapse between completion of a study and publication, or when the data become stale.

The procedural-traditional view of time is evident in peer review processes. Journal articles and book manuscripts can go through several revisions before they are ready for publication, and the finished product must meet a normative standard. The process of article submission and review is quite open-ended. One submits work when he or she thinks it is finished and others judge whether it is completed. People may try to segment their work to maximize the number of publications during an academic year, but they risk being told that parts of an article are missing or that they should wait until they have results to report.

As mentioned earlier, a distinction can be made between the temporal aspects of discrete research projects, especially those that are sponsored, and programs of scholarship discussed in the section on campus culture. Outside agencies organize their years into relevant temporal units—fiscal years—and they often organize their activities into funding cycles. A faculty member must be responsive to the temporal dimension of these cultures in order to stay in phase with funding schedules. In instances where research is sponsored and faculty have committed to a particular sequence of project activities, the calendar and clock are also key determinants of the rhythm, pace, and intensity of work.

Clearly there are other time-related norms within discipline cultures that might be discussed, such as when in their careers faculty members are likely to do their best work. However, this brief overview establishes that it is valid to speak of a temporal dimension of discipline norms. These time-linked expectations may occasionally be at odds with campus norms. Within any defined unit of time, the pattern of faculty work activities may be attributable to normative pressures in a single or several organizational cultures, both on and off campus.

Implications for Defining Workload. Workload takes on different meanings when viewed from these three cultural perspectives. The linear-segmental view of time fits with definitions that break activities into calendar- and clock-based time units and assign monetary values to these units. Production units can be hours of instruction, number of students graduating, or number of publications. Within the circular-traditional framework, the relevant temporal unit would not be calendar-dependent but grounded in past experience with instruction or scholarship. Productivity cycles would be defined in ways that are relevant to the activities themselves and responsive to the conditions that prevail within the organization. Consider as an example a department that is undergoing a major curricular revision; there are likely to be disruptions in environmental conditions that were previously under faculty control. Among administrators and researchers with a circular-traditional perspective of time, these disruptions would be taken into account as productivity of faculty during this period is assessed, and the assessment of the curricular revision would be timed to coincide with phases in its development, not necessarily the academic or calendar year. Similarly, scholarly productivity would be assessed in cycles that fit the disciplinary norms, with some disciplines continuing to use the year as the temporal unit, and others, perhaps history or philosophy, using a different time frame due to the nature of the scholarly process.

If workload were viewed from the procedural-linear perspective, the focus would be put clearly on the quality of outcomes, and shift away from duration of activity as traditionally defined in Western culture. Among individuals who share this view of time, normative standards of quality determine when an activity is completed, not a calendar or clock, and they would likely argue that college campuses must be prepared to think about the assessment of teaching performance in terms of students' accomplishment of standards. Duration of study may vary across students and subject areas; some might conform to the academic term but others may take longer. Arrangements must be made for faculty to work with students who fall behind and flexibility in course length becomes essential. Similarly, faculty productivity must be defined in terms of the quality of course content and instruction as well as how a faculty member's students perform in upper-division courses, how many gain admission to graduate school, their performance at their place of employment, and so forth. If this view of time prevails, students and administrators must accustom themselves to a more open-ended process of teaching and learning. Setting the standards would become the primary task.

In terms of scholarship, the critical message from those who adhere to a procedural-linear concept of time is that quality of publications—their impact on the field—should replace annual yield as the primary indicator of productivity.

From this perspective, trivial publications have more to do with efforts to legislate production schedules by those who hold a linear-segmental view of time and want standardized units across fields, and less to do with the research model per se, as argued by some writers (Heydinger and Simsek, 1992).

At the individual level, the literature on cultural orientations to time underscores the importance of understanding the multiple normative contexts within which faculty work. We must ask, In what ways do the temporal aspects of norms within different cultures create pressures that foster or hinder faculty productivity? The image of the professor with complete autonomy over her or his work is inaccurate. Faculty must constantly balance multiple time-related expectations in order to be productive. Most faculty members' work activities must be synchronized. There may be instances when competing norms have a negative effect on this synchronization and reduce certain types of productivity; as noted earlier, discipline norms for publication can be in conflict with campus expectations. However, there are also instances where consistency in norms fosters the kind of pressure that enhances productivity, as when college pressure to complete a curricular revision within a particular time frame results in coordinated effort among department faculty. When drawing comparisons between faculty and other professions, we must take into account the fact that individuals who do not simultaneously practice their profession and teach in a college setting are not working in the same kind of normative context.

How Faculty Experience Time

The previous section dealt with the cultural aspects of time. However, another aspect is also important to research on workload, namely individual perceptions of time (Flaherty, 1991). The research on faculty workload has consistently shown that professors' estimates of the number of hours they work are always higher than estimates made by observers (Yuker, 1984). Research on time perception helps explain the discrepancies and adds to our understanding of why faculty believe studies of their work habits present distorted portraits.

To comprehend how faculty perceive time, I asked several colleagues how they experience time and how they thought their experience of time differs from that of other people. Almost everyone made it clear that they never had enough time to do everything. They spoke of how difficult it was to find the blocks of time needed for activities such as course preparation and writing. They also noted that they thought the way they experienced time and how others assumed they used time were quite different. They reported that autonomy with respect to managing time did not translate into an easy job; there were real constraints and pressures to produce that were not evident to the outside observer but regulated how they used unscheduled time. They talked about the difficulty of juggling different activities and the felt pressures when calendar deadlines for proposals, conference papers, and grades were upon them, personal deadlines for projects came into conflict with unanticipated roadblocks, or responsibilities on campus burgeoned out of control. Contrary to what they thought was the public's impression, they felt they fit their scholarship around instruction-related activities (classes, supervision of dissertations, and advising).

Woven through their comments were observations about the different cultures in which they worked and cases where the time demands came into conflict. For example, they noted how the set schedule for ongoing teaching and administrative responsibilities made it difficult to respond to requests for proposals that had short lead times. This problem became critical when not submitting meant they must wait through a full funding cycle. They commented on how much easier it would be to borrow time and immerse themselves in preparing an application in an organization where research was the sole activity. They were frustrated by nonacademic organizations that were not familiar with the rhythm of life on campus and that scheduled meetings or established deadlines at times when activities were fast-paced and intense. At times, this made them feel that there was an implied message that academic researchers need not apply. They also spoke of unreasonable deadlines established by campus administrators who had no instructional responsibilities or experience. In short, they conveyed a clear sense of exasperation with the lack of sensitivity on the part of some decision makers to the temporal dimension of norms outside of their own culture.

When they elaborated on their personal experiences of time, their comments fit with the research on the impact of stimulus intensity and individual engrossment on perceptions of time. Flaherty (1991) explains that time as measured by the clock and as experienced can be in synchrony; that is, the estimate of elapsed time and actual clock measured time are the same. He points out, however, that there are cases when experienced time and standard temporal units are not aligned. He quotes Csikszentmihalyi's writing on the subjective estimates of time to illustrate when people underestimate measured time: "people who enjoy what they are doing enter in a state of 'flow': they concentrate their attention on a limited stimulus field, forget personal problems, lose their sense of time and themselves, feel competent and in control, and have a sense of harmony and union with their surroundings" (p. 182).

Flaherty's own research focuses on instances where the experience of time is protracted; people overestimate the time that passed. He assumed that time viewed by outsiders as busy would seem to pass more quickly and unfilled time would seem to move slowly. However, he found that people overestimated the time at both ends of this continuum. He offered a tentative explanation for this phenomenon that stressed the importance of stimulus complexity and individual engrossment in the situation, a concept that is closely related to the concept of tempo intensity discussed earlier. In short, Flaherty found that what appeared to observers to be uneventful and unfilled periods of time could have high stimulus complexity for the participant. For example, a woman on the first day of work in an all-male business reported that the longest minute of her life occurred when she walked into the waiting area and no one said a word, just stared. It felt as if she stood there for hours, even though it was only minutes before she actually reached her desk. She was engrossed in her situation and found it to be filled with activity.

My colleagues shared their feelings of when they were "in the flow," and were likely to underestimate the amount of clock time. One professor said, "I am unaware of time passing when my writing is going well, or I am making progress toward the solution of a problem." Another colleague noted, "When I am writing or working on a computer program, I am consumed. It is a creative period, total immersion. I lose track of time when I am working on multiple embedded problems and I am making progress." Yet another faculty member described a similar perception of time when her teaching was going well. "I sometimes realize that I don't know where the time went when we are having a good exchange of ideas, when students are excited about topics." These comments illustrate the fact that for these faculty, time flies when things are going smoothly and they are engrossed in their work. Estimations of workload may vary depending on this sense of success and the meaningfulness of the activity.

On the other hand, there are cases where people are engrossed but time seems to drag. A poorly executed assignment can seem to take an extraordinary amount of time to correct, even if the lapsed clock time says otherwise. An exemplary paper, likewise, can seem to take a long time to grade. In both cases, the faculty member may overestimate how much time was spent on the activity due to the stimulus complexity. Flaherty argues that we develop expectations of the "density of experience per temporal unit" (1991, p. 84) and we structure our allocations of time to activities around these expectations. We come to expect that we will need to carry out a set of activities tailored to grading a particular type of paper and that they will take a certain amount of time. In the case of a poorly written paper, the stimulus complexity is higher than expected because the paper is riddled with multiple embedded problems; the density of the actual experience surpasses what was foreseen. In the second, because the content is rich the stimulus complexity is greater than anticipated. Faculty experience with such instructional activities probably contributes to their skepticism about attempts to standardize the time allocated to their activities as well as to their inflation of work time estimates.

The respondents' comments also elicited some insights as to how individual differences in social and psychological characteristics can affect experienced time. One colleague (referring to me) observed, "My sense of when something is finished is different from yours. For me, it is when I think it's good enough for others to respond to. For you, it has to be perfect, complete!" In essence, he was saying that we differed in how we bring activities to closure, an individual characteristic that contributes to our perceptions of how long it takes us to complete the same activity. A senior faculty member reported, "I am not driven by ambition to the extent many of my colleagues are. I do not have the pressing need for national recognition, to promote myself, that is part of some colleagues' make-up. Nor do I have the need to be promoted by others as is the case of the junior faculty." He then went on to say that he thought he was less aware of the passing of time when compared with his colleagues who had this drive or those who were untenured.

A junior faculty member explained how the pressure to produce imposed by the institution differed from the self-induced pressure felt by tenured colleagues and how this difference affected her. She said, "I would do everything I am doing now anyway, but the fact that the university says I have to produce makes me angry. I hate to have to. . . . My work will always be an integral part of my life, by choice." This external pressure in her view led to a compressed feeling of time, that there really never was enough time to do everything that was expected and that it was "dangerous to be off schedule."

Pressures such as these may derive from two kinds of overload. In their study of the workload of university professors, French, Tupper, and Mueller (1965) distinguished between calling on a particular ability too heavily (quantitative overload) and calling on abilities that are not possessed (qualitative overload). Faculty comments were laced with examples of quantitative overload but one was particularly illustrative. A colleague said, "I'm not sure how I should feel about working with people I'm not really connected to in any way . . . people I don't really know but who drop in for consultation . . . they place demands on my time that don't fall within any of my roles— as teacher, or researcher. How am I supposed to account for or count this time?"

Qualitative overload is often experienced by faculty when they do things for the first time, such as teaching, preparing a grant proposal, or chairing a dissertation. One first-year professor teaching three courses (all for the first time) talked about how this demand taxed one's teaching ability. This person noted that the gap between organizational demands and knowledge about teaching (qualitative overload) led to quantitative overload in the research area as well: time that would have been given to research had to be reallocated to teaching, an observation that is consistent with the findings of French, Tupper, and Mueller.

French and his colleagues found that faculty reports of quantitative overload were higher among individuals who were also high in achievement orientation (an orientation to one's profession that emphasizes esteem in the eyes of the public that is achieved through one's work). This finding fits nicely with the earlier observation about individual differences in experienced time that might be attributable to one's need for self-promotion. Faculty whom my colleague described as "motivated by self-promotion" may be more aware of time because of quantitative overload. This pressure could skew estimates of work time so that they are higher than those of outside observers.

Implications for Studies of Workload

One clear implication for policy makers is to take care in interpreting observers' reports of faculty workload. Flaherty (1991, p. 82) notes, "Where human experience is concerned, standard units of temporality that seem uneventful to the detached observer may actually encompass a wealth of emotional and cognitive processes on the part of those involved subjectively with their circumstances." Perhaps one area in which we ought to begin research on experienced time among faculty is in those areas where they and observers differ in their estimations of work time. Studies of this type would enable us to identify activities that are experienced as longer in duration and could help explain why this is so. This explanation, in turn, might help higher educators describe faculty work in ways that communicate to the public the complexity of their activities.

Another contribution of this line of research is the distinction between qualitative and quantitative overload. Administrators, policy makers, and higher education researchers ought to distinguish those aspects of workload that may require adjustment in terms of the number of demands on faculty time from those that require support for faculty who need to enhance their skills in certain areas.

I noted at the beginning of this chapter that little research has been done regarding organizational perspectives of time and their impact on work activity patterns. I have argued that the social constructions of time that are relevant to college administrators, policy makers, or other professionals may not always be applicable to faculty work. If these basic temporal units are inappropriate, they may mitigate against productivity in general as well as against work quality. Resolving this difficult problem will be an essential first step in redefining faculty workload and productivity. The concern raised thirty years ago by French and his colleagues seems even more important today: "The tendency seems to be today to transform the university into a business concern that delivers a product: knowledge. It seems that putting on pressure and creating overload have been successful in making the university a 'going concern' whose stock is rising. But what did we lose, and, if we lost something, can we afford to lose it?" (p. 148).

References

Clark, B. "The Academic Life—Small Worlds, Different Worlds." *Educational Researcher*, 1989, *18* (5), 4–8.

Flaherty, M. G. "The Perception of Time and Situated Engrossment." *Social Psychology Quarterly*, 1991, *54* (1), 76–85.

French, J. R., Jr., Tupper, J. C., and Mueller, E. F. *Work Load of University Professors*. Ann Arbor: Institute for Social Research, The University of Michigan, 1965.

Graham, R. "The Role of Perception of Time in Consumer Research." *Journal of Consumer Research*, 1981, *7*, 335–342.

Heydinger, R. B., and Simsek, H. *An Agenda for Reshaping Faculty Productivity*. Denver: State Higher Education Executive Offices, 1992.

Lauer, R. *Temporal Man: The Meaning and Social Uses of Time*. New York: Praeger, 1981.

Light, D. W., Jr. "Introduction: The Structure of the Academic Professions." *Sociology of Education*, 1974, 47 (1), 18.

Lim, Y. M., and Seers, A. "Time Dimensions of Work: Relationships with Perceived Organizational Performance." *Journal of Business and Psychology*, 1993, 8 (1), 91–102.

Owen, A. J. "Time and Time Again: Implications of Time Perception Theory." *Lifestyles: Family and Economic Issues*. 1991, 12 (4), 345–359.

Parsons, T., and Platt, G. *The American University*. Cambridge, Mass.: Harvard University Press, 1973.

Schriber, J. B., and Gutek, B. A. "Some Time Dimensions of Work: Measurement of an Underlying Aspect of Organization Culture." *Journal of Applied Psychology*, 1987, 72 (4), 642–650.

Tierney, W. "Academic Work and Institutional Culture." *The Review of Higher Education*, 1991, 14 (2), 199–216.

Yuker, H. E. *Faculty Workload: Research, Theory, and Interpretation*. Washington, D.C.: ASHE-ERIC Higher Education Research Report No. 10, 1984.

JANET H. LAWRENCE is associate professor in the Center for the Study of Higher and Postsecondary Education and Associate Dean of the School of Education at the University of Michigan.

Workload initiatives and productivity expectations can be used to help chart future directions.

Approaches to Conducting Faculty Workload Studies: A Case Study at Kent State University

Greer Glazer, Myron S. Henry

The main purposes of this chapter are to discuss workload initiatives at Kent State University during the last two and a half years and to describe how the several initiatives are interdependent. Particular attention is given to the important and pervasive role of an expanded view of scholarship in faculty workload and productivity. Although the workload initiatives discussed in this chapter may not be unique, in combination they redefine and extend traditional approaches to faculty workload and productivity. As other colleges and universities develop workload initiatives tailored to their circumstances, they may benefit not only from the workload studies described below, but also from the challenges Kent has experienced in moving from initiatives to practices.

Institutional Context

The issue of faculty workload is inextricably linked to faculty productivity expectations including what constitutes faculty scholarship. Although the national expectations of academic disciplines and professions play the main role in defining scholarship, reconsideration of scholarship within the context of missions of colleges universities is occurring across the country (Boyer, 1990). Kent State University is a large institution with a complex mission. Approximately 33,000 students are enrolled at its eight northeast Ohio campuses, including nearly 23,000 at its Kent Campus. Doctoral degrees are awarded in twenty-one distinct academic fields and significant sponsored program activity is evident in selected research areas. Kent is not a traditional research university, but does characterize itself as a research-oriented university. Like other large, complex universities, Kent State has acknowledged the importance of reexamining its multifaceted mission, reaffirming its historical commitment to providing a superb undergraduate education, and recognizing the multiple roles and responsibilities of faculty. The need to analyze, measure, and redefine what constitutes faculty workload and productivity expectations at Kent has been motivated and facilitated by a number of factors and initiatives.

Almost immediately after her appointment in the spring of 1992 as the tenth president of Kent State University, Carol A. Cartwright began the dialogue on faculty roles, productivity, and rewards. In her inaugural address, Cartwright indicated that she intended to initiate a process for the reconceptualization of scholarship at Kent. With encouragement from the president, the faculty senate took the lead role in the reconsideration of scholarship when it established the Commission on Scholarship in December of 1991. Cartwright also initiated a pilot study on the complexities of faculty workload and productivity involving six major academic units, a study that was later extended in modified form to most of the university's departments and schools. In the summer of 1993, the University Priorities and Budget Advisory Committee (UPBAC), a widely representative committee appointed by the president and chaired by the provost, undertook the development of a document that was to capsulize the defining features of Kent State University. This document, the Kent Institutional Characteristics (KICS) statement, embraces a more encompassing sense of scholarship as a main defining feature of Kent State University. Almost simultaneously, UPBAC considered a quantitative model prepared by the Provost's Office that proposed department- and school-specific student–faculty ratios by levels of instruction as one important aspect of unit workload and overall productivity.

Two other major initiatives at Kent have reaffirmed and refined all of these efforts at workload redefinition. First, the university became one of thirty participants in a major national effort supported by the Pew Charitable Trusts to examine the academic department as the principal unit for implementing change. A twenty-five-person Kent Pew Roundtable developed a major position paper on five issues basic to the future progress of the university. Second, the university began a major strategic planning process guided by the *Kent Institutional Characteristics* statement. These two important initiatives have provided opportunities for the university to refine and further develop its notions of an expanded view of scholarship, faculty workload, and overall unit productivity.

The pace of initiatives at Kent has been influenced by events external to the university. In particular, a budget shortfall in Ohio in fiscal years 1993 and 1994 resulted in reductions in state subsidy to Kent of approximately 15 percent (about $11 million) during the two-year period. At about the same time, the Ohio Board of Regents convened the Managing for the Future Task Force (MFTFTF) to conduct a statewide study and make recommendations for restructuring and improving higher education in Ohio. Many of these recommendations ultimately dealt with faculty roles, workload, and productivity. To implement selected MFTFTF recommendations, the Ohio Board of Regents issued its own report, *Securing the Future of Higher Education in Ohio,* and then commissioned several special-purpose state-level implementation committees. Some of these committees have dealt or are dealing with faculty roles, workload, productivity, and rewards. Language mandating a 10 percent increase in statewide undergraduate teaching activity was incorporated into the 1994 budget bill for higher education in Ohio.

There has been much activity in Ohio and at Kent State University during the last two and a half years on faculty roles, workload, productivity, and rewards. The sections that follow provide more detail on workload related initiatives; describe process, challenges, and progress in connecting these interdependent initiatives; and project future directions emanating from workload studies and productivity expectations.

Faculty Senate Commission on Scholarship. The Commission on Scholarship was established to consider whether the approach advocated by Ernest Boyer in his 1990 book *Scholarship Reconsidered* (or some modification of it) is consistent with the faculty's conceptualization of scholarship; can be made concrete enough to be useful to faculty; could be used as a framework for merit, promotion, and tenure decisions; and might be part of a redesign of program evaluation.

The five-person commission, with members from the School of Nursing and the departments of sociology, music, physics, adult education, counseling education, health education, and vocational education, began what would be nearly a year of study, consultation, and deliberation. The commission issued its report on the nature of scholarship at Kent State in December 1992. In the spirit of Boyer's landmark work, the commission's report advocated that Kent State University embrace a more encompassing definition of scholarship so that the breadth of faculty interests and talents are better used and recognized.

After much debate and input, the faculty senate adopted the commission's *Principles for the Evaluation and Reward of Faculty Scholarship,* which included twenty principles for reconceptualizing scholarship around discovery, teaching, application, and integration as formulated by Boyer. The principles also included operational statements that encouraged departments and schools to embark on reviews and revisions in their procedures to ensure that the more encompassing interpretations of scholarship are properly recognized, fostered, evaluated, and rewarded. To illustrate their nature, six of the principles most directly related to faculty workload and performance evaluation follow.

There must be consistency and clarity in defining criteria indicative of the types of scholarship.
The issue of the quality of all types of scholarships must be addressed by each department and school.

All four aspects of scholarship must be considered and rewarded at the department and school levels.

Criteria should respond fully to the diverse aspects of faculty roles.

Weighting of criteria may differ for faculty with differential roles and rank.

A threshold of good citizenship (service activities not necessarily tied directly to one's special field of knowledge) should be established by each department and be required of all faculty.

Recognizing that the key to implementing the twenty principles rests with how they are interpreted at department and school levels, the provost and chair of the faculty senate volunteered to meet with department and school faculty in town-meeting formats to discuss the principles and their implementation. Each department and school was asked to prepare a short plan in which it interpreted the principles within its own context and discussed how it would implement them.

The missions of the thirty-seven departments and schools at Kent display considerable variability, and the definition of what constitutes scholarship has always been a broad one. Thus the responses by departments and schools to the twenty principles have varied from "We already do this," to "Here is how we think the principles apply to us, how we intend to change, and what we think we will achieve," to "Why should we do this?," to no response so far. As an illustration of the range of responses, the department of philosophy, which does not offer a Ph.D. degree, interpreted the principles in imaginative ways, indicated how it evaluates the various forms of scholarship, attempted to show how the scholarships are related, and concluded that it is already achieving the purposes of the principles. In one of the most innovative responses, the department of biological sciences, a Ph.D.-granting department with considerable sponsored program activity, cast the four Boyer types of scholarship within the traditional categories of teaching, research, and service. Specific examples of the scholarships of teaching, discovery, integration, and application viewed within the teaching, research, and service categories were quite novel.

Many departments and schools have yet to respond to the request that they interpret the twenty principles within their own contexts. In conjunction with Kent Pew Roundtable and strategic planning initiatives, the provost's office and faculty senate will renew requests that departments and schools prepare brief plans for the interpretation and implementation of the twenty principles. As the plans are developed and endorsed, they will become key ingredients to faculty workloads and productivity expectations.

The work of the commission and the faculty senate, as well as *The Principles for the Evaluation and Reward of Scholarship,* helped pave the way for the emphasis on an expanded view of scholarship that appears in the *Kent Institutional Characteristics* statement and the strategic plan.

Kent Institutional Characteristics and Strategic Plan. The Kent Institutional Characteristics (KICS) statement, a principal defining document for Kent State

University, embraces an extended view of scholarship as a significant feature in the professional lives of Kent faculty, and thereby reinforces the efforts of the faculty senate to promote a broad view of scholarship. The University Priorities and Budget Advisory Committee (UPBAC), a widely representative, twenty-five person committee, began work on the statement in the summer of 1992. The KICS statement interprets and expands on the Kent State University role and mission statement under eleven thematic categories: students, faculty, curriculum, special features, teaching, research and creative activity, outreach and community service, campus environment and cocurricular activities, diversity, alumni, and evaluation. Although the KICS statement does not specifically reference faculty workload, it does reinforce the concept of "scholarship extended" and therefore implicitly helps to frame faculty workloads and performance expectations. For example, the statement "To promote learning and foster the intellectual life of the University, Kent seeks to attract and retain active, culturally and academically diverse faculty of the highest caliber, skilled in the scholarship of teaching, discovery, application, and integration" (KICS) expands the concept of scholarship beyond traditional interpretations.

The process culminating in the KICS statement set the stage for an even more ambitious effort. Specifically, in late summer 1993, Kent State University embarked on an extensive and inclusive strategic planning process motivated in part by mandates from the Ohio Board of Regents; guided by the Kent Institutional Characteristics statement; based on department, school, college, and divisional strategic plans; and ultimately endorsed by the Board of Trustees of Kent State University. Sections of the academic and student affairs part of this strategic plan address faculty workload and productivity expectations, and reaffirm and expand on workload issues described in other Kent State University documents. For example, the following goal is contained in the strategic plan: "Refine faculty workload policies at the department and school levels so that they better reflect the multifaceted nature of faculty scholarship and responsibilities."

Two of the objectives to this goal state, "Continue developing departmental workload policies which address specific unit contributions to the University mission," and "Maintain a workload policy that is comparable to those in force in similar research-oriented institutions while responding constructively to recently established state mandates."

The strategic plan also reinforces Kent Pew Roundtable principles on workload and productivity. For example, one goal states, "Foster departmental/ school productivity through the concepts of teamwork, unit productivity, and group rewards."

The summary chapter contains the statement "this strategic plan has stressed the interconnected, mutually supportive, and complementary nature of units and functions at Kent State University." As the most important direction-setting document for the university for the next several years, the strategic plan sets a stage for further development and refinement of faculty responsibilities, workload, and productivity expectations in the context of the individual and the unit.

Faculty Workload Study

In the fall of 1992 President Cartwright asked Lynette Andresen, an American Council on Education (ACE) Fellow at Kent, to lead a pilot study on faculty workload in six Kent State University academic units. The faculty workload study piloted a new approach to evaluating faculty contributions by using the academic department (school) as the unit of analysis in contrast to analyzing the activities of individual faculty members. This study was singled out by the Ohio Board of Regents as a "best practice" for analyzing faculty workloads and productivity.

The six participating units were representative of the breadth of academic missions present at the university. One unit, the department of physics, offers the Ph.D. degree and engages in considerable sponsored program activity. The School of Nursing is a master's level unit with major clinical responsibilities. The department of english, Kent's largest department, offers the Ph.D. degree. This department also has a major leadership role in the delivery of the university's liberal education requirements and serves large numbers of students in lower division composition courses. The School of Art has many majors and offers the terminal M.F.A. degree. The Salem Regional Campus offers two-year associate degrees to place-bound students in rural northeast Ohio and a full spectrum of first- and second-year general education courses to students who may aspire to a baccalaureate degree from Kent State University. The department of psychology is the leader among Kent's social and behavior sciences departments in numbers of undergraduate majors, Ph.D. students, and sponsored program activity.

Faculty Productivity Worksheets. Faculty in participating units completed a faculty productivity worksheet that generated a weekly accounting of time spent on professional responsibilities, including scholarly activities. They responded to questions about the number of hours they spent engaged in the various types of professional activities (teaching, research and creative activities, and professional and public service). Thus, the faculty productivity worksheet basically consisted of a matrix with days of the week as columns, and with rows identified by types of activities under the broad categories of scholarship, teaching, academic advising, and administrative functions. The scholarship category posed questions in terms of Boyer's (1990) definitions. The teaching category included the myriad of activities that constitute instruction (such as classroom instruction, clinical instruction, counseling of students, office hours, student evaluation, course preparation, and advising). Under the broad teaching category, faculty could register their instructional activities within any of forty separate categories. An abbreviated version of the faculty productivity worksheet appears in Exhibit 4.1.

Exhibit 4.1. Faculty Productivity Worksheet

I. **Scholarship**

  A. **Research:** What is to be known, what is yet to be found? (Boyer definition)

    Examples: Grant writing and administration, research-writing (include software), read research literature, referee articles and present papers, creative activity.

Hours per Week

M	T	W	TH	F	SA	SU	Total

Comments:

  B. **Integration:** What do the research findings mean? Making connections across the disciplines, fitting research into larger intellectual patterns (Boyer's definition).

    Examples: Interdisciplinary activities, general education activities, collaborative activities, topical or problem-centered activities, writing of textbooks, department colloquia, conference attendance.

  C. **Application:** How can knowledge be responsibly applied to consequential problems? Knowledge that arises out of the very act of application, whether in serving clients in psychotherapy, shaping public policy, creating an architectural design, or working with the public schools (Boyer's definition).

    Examples: Community projects and activities (speeches, interviews), clinical practice and services (give number served), corporate activities, state- and federally funded activities (other than research), consulting, performances and exhibitions, K–12 activities, other expertise-driven activities that are of service to community.

  D. **Teaching:** The planning and examination of pedagogical procedures (Boyer's definition).

    Examples: Curriculum development, faculty training and mentoring, oversight of graduate assistants, activities involving how to teach (history as biography), activities involving teaching effectiveness (how students learn material).

Total Hours per Week All Scholarship Activities

M	T	W	TH	F	SA	SU	Total

Exhibit 4.1. (*continued*)

II. **Instruction**

A. **Classroom Instruction:** Faculty indicated also the number of courses and students enrolled in each course for each classification

Hours per Week

	M	T	W	TH	F	SA	SU	Total
LER courses								
Service courses								
Major courses								
Other undergraduate courses								
Graduate major courses								
Other graduate courses								

Faculty were also asked to complete similar charts for these categories: B. **Laboratory instruction**; C. **Clinical supervision**; D. **Studio and performance-exhibition supervision**; E. **Individualized instruction**; F. **Class preparation** (including review of literature for current and future courses, syllabus preparation, creation and review of lesson plan and notes, preparation for use of A/V and computer equipment); G. **Evaluation of student work** (including preparation, administration, and grading of examinations and laboratory reports, review of clinical work, review of creative work); H. **Other student contact** (including course review instructions, reviews of examinations with students, and contacts during office hours). There was also a chart to record hours spent per week in I. **Travel time** (for intercampus instruction). The **Instruction** category concluded with the following chart.

Total Hours per Week for All Instructional Activities

M	T	W	TH	F	SA	SU	Total

Other major categories on the form were **Academic Advising** and **Administrative** duties.

III. **Academic Advising:** Includes program, course, graduate school, and career advising and writing of letters of recommendation. Does not include activities identified in II. H.

Function				**Hours per Week**				
	M	T	W	TH	F	SA	SU	Total

Comments:

Exhibit 4.1. (*continued*)

IV. **Administrative**
   A. **Department**
   Examples: Committees (governance, recruitment, fundraising, travel time for inter-campus meetings).

Hours per Week

M	T	W	TH	F	SA	SU	Total

Comments:

Additional categories under the **Administrative** heading with examples in paren-theses were B. **College**; C. **University**; D. **Professional, Discipline, Higher Education** (professional association officer, reading and taking courses to keep up with profession); and E. **Regulatory** (State and federal mandates such as assessment, human subjects review, radiation safety, and accreditation activities).

Total Hours per Week for All Administrative Activities

M	T	W	TH	F	SA	SU	Total

The faculty productivity worksheet concluded with a chart for the number of hours spent per week for all of the categories and activities outlined above.

Although the faculty productivity worksheet provided very useful information, the response rate from faculty was low for several of the six units. Probable reasons for the limited number of responses to the form are its length and the amount of detail requested. To further validate the conclusions based on the collective responses to the faculty productivity worksheets, the provost's office asked faculty in five of the six study units to complete a one-page, numerically based survey that included questions on the major categories of the faculty productivity worksheet. The response rate from faculty in the participating units for this short-form survey was high, and the results were fully consistent with those observed from tabulating the responses to the faculty productivity worksheet. Copies of the complete faculty productivity worksheet and the short-form survey are available from the authors.

Weekly Faculty Logs. One of the most informative aspects of the faculty workload study involved three faculty in each of the six participating units. Specifically, these faculty were asked to keep written logs or diaries of professional activities for one week. The resulting logs were quite varied in nature, but each demonstrated the diversity of professional activities faculty engaged in during an average week. Descriptions of faculty activities ranged from a mere listing of all activities encountered during the test week to full written explanations of how particular activities related to the four types of scholarship. Logs that included linkages between scholarship and other professional activities were most helpful in gaining further insight into the complexities of faculty professional work. The excerpts that follow were taken from five days' entries in the log of one faculty member from the School of Nursing.

> *Wednesday, March 11, 1992.* I arrived at the School of Nursing on the Kent Campus at 8:30 A.M. to an overwhelming amount of mail. My morning was filled with a potpourri of activities. I began by reading articles on faculty productivity and workload. These were perused in preparation for my role as chair of the Faculty Senate Commission on Scholarship. As chair of the School of Nursing Graduate Curriculum Committee, I then made faculty assignments to four new subcommittees that were created as a result of our recent Graduate Curriculum Retreat. Since our next meeting was the following week, I prepared the agenda and accompanying materials. I then reviewed a letter I had drafted to be sent to a colleague that was facilitating research I was interested in doing on African American women. Four phone calls were made, including two return calls to the Graduate College Curriculum Committee (I am a member) and one to the university media department that wanted to know about a political action award I had received in the fall. A student concerned about her name's absence on our fall class list had left a note in my absence, so I followed up on this with our administrators. A faculty member came to my office to ask about her request to be named to the Public Health Council by Ohio Nursing Association. I spoke with her about the process and encouraged future attempts for membership on other committees. The latter part of the morning was spent reading and commenting upon student clinical logs. One student's clinical experience involved a client being induced for labor with prostaglandin gel. I was able to provide significant input into this case since I was primary author on an article in a refereed nursing journal on this topic. I also graded a paper on the student's personal theoretical model of nursing. Since I had spent 2-1/2 hours with this student at my house the previous week, I was gratified to see that my suggestions were incorporated into the paper. The student's grade on two papers was B+ as compared to a C on her last paper. My awareness of the significance that this paper would have on the student led to my calling the student at home to inform her of the grade and express my congratulations on her improvement.
>
> My afternoon began with a meeting with a research assistant assigned to assist me with my current research project. I am investigating "Predictors, moderators, and health outcomes of the transition to midlife for White and African American Women." This is an outgrowth of previous

work with menopausal women and the concepts of stress and anxiety. This current project is being done to serve as pilot data for submission of an Academic Investigator Award in the near future. The Case Western Reserve University Alumni Fund has provided $1,000 mainly to pay each of the 160 subjects $5 for completing the questionnaires. Preplanning discussions with the Cleveland Chapter of the Black Nurses Association suggested money as incentive to encourage subject participation. The meeting with the GA centered on assembling the packets of questionnaires to give to subjects, developing a code book, and idea generation for entree into sites for data collection. My meeting was only interrupted once for a phone call with the co-instructor of the course I missed on Tuesday. We discussed the prior class session, student papers, and next week's class. The Faculty Senate Commission on Scholarship (which I chair) met from 1:30–3:30. The meeting focused on what might be considered as evidence of the four types of scholarship proposed by Boyer. A matrix was developed and critiqued, and the remaining time was spent discussing the evolving principles of the model for reconceptualizing scholarship. We are making good progress and will have something concrete for faculty response. One commission member stayed after the meeting for one-half hour to continue discussion on the guidelines and the matrix. Since the commission work was fresh in my mind, I spent the next one hour revising the matrix and guidelines so they would be available prior to the next meeting. My day at Kent ended by returning a phone call to a lawyer for whom I serve as an expert witness in a medical malpractice case. We discussed the case for approximately fifteen minutes. Later in the evening and after I had spent 2-1/2 hours of "quality" time with my three children, I settled down to prepare for next week's class discussion on support groups. Approximately four hours were spent reviewing prior class notes, reading new articles, reviewing other articles and book chapters, and planning strategies for the delivery of the material. I developed an outline of key points I wanted to make sure were covered, but planned to let students take the lead in pursuing their interests since each was required to read at least three articles of their choice.

Thursday, March 12. I met my student at 8:15 A.M. at the British Petroleum station on Chagrin Boulevard in Cleveland because I was going to a clinical site with which I was unfamiliar. In fact, the clinical site is an Iwason House in the City of Cleveland. Iwason is a treatment center for pregnant women with substance abuse problems. This clinical site was deliberately chosen for the specific student because she wants to develop expertise with pregnant women who abuse cocaine and their children. Her first clinical experience last semester was at a children's hospital with women who had a positive drug screen at birth and were being studied at a special clinic for their babies. A goal today was to evaluate a teaching session my student had developed focusing on the last trimester of pregnancy. I already had commented on the written teaching plan. I also wanted to see how she was incorporating an advanced nursing intervention (humor) that she had chosen to focus on this semester. The student did a remarkable job although her preceptor, an employee at Iwason, constantly interrupted. After the teaching session I was able to talk with the student and preceptor about my perceptions including the interruptions by the preceptor. The teaching session became a support group after a while and this was discussed. A major shortcoming of the treatment as identified by me was the focus on the individual to the exclusion of significant others. The student will follow up on this. I also observed my student provide a physical assessment and ongoing discussion with the client she is following during the semester. Suggestions related to technique and follow-up were provided. As a result of my supervision, I suggested that the student attend the labor and delivery, and develop a care plan for the client for her hospitalization so that her client would receive the best available care. Due to my prior clinical experience, I could foresee many issues related to pain, medication, support people in labor, mother child bonding and child care that would be dealt with best by anticipating guidance and care planning. The experience at Iwason extended until 1:30 P.M., whereupon the student and I went to lunch and talked about the clinical experience as well as her future plans.

Since I already was in the neighborhood of a colleague, I went to an African American nurse's house who had promised to assist me with data collection for my research project. We reviewed the data collection procedure, I gave her ten questionnaire packets, and she supplied me with names of other African American nurses who might help me with data collection. I was grateful for her assistance and looked forward to the receipt of the subjects' questionnaires. I could hardly wait to call her friends for help.

I managed to call my husband at 4:30 P.M. to report on my day. When I returned home, I played with my children until 9:00 P.M. From then until midnight, I worked on the Academic Investigator grant that I plan to submit in June. Admittedly, it's hard to get back to grant writing when I've had such a lengthy layoff from that. However, I read the Dilman book (a must) on questionnaire development and incorporated many ideas into the design of my questionnaire and method section.

Friday, March 13. Starting at 9:00 A.M., I read my mail. At 9:30 A.M., I met with a student for one hour to discuss our research presentation on the Experience of Terminal Illness in Adolescence to be presented at the March 30 Midwest Nursing Research Society (MNRS) meeting in Chicago. The MNRS meeting is one of the top nursing research conferences in the country. By the conclusion of the meeting the student had the material to bring to the Audio Visual Department to make the slides we need for the conference. A ride to Akron with my dean followed in which discussion ensued on various issues at the School as well as the Graduate College Curriculum Committee. The doctoral task force members from Kent and Akron University met from 11:00 A.M. to 3:00 P.M. to discuss and refine the curriculum plan for our consortial Ph.D. program. Our meeting concluded with general consensus about the major curriculum content and number of required credit hours. A sense of accomplishment and pride is present as this dream moves a step forward to becoming a reality.

After riding back with the dean, I met with the chair of the Faculty Senate. He had asked me to consider running for chair, and I asked to meet with him to learn more about the time commitment I would be making. He assured me that my commitment wouldn't be much more than my present commitment as member of the Senate. While I agreed to be a candidate, this decision was not without reservations, particularly since I am scheduled to teach two five-credit clinical courses in the fall and intend to continue pursuit of my research.

Saturday, March 14. I finally had uninterrupted time for writing on my Academic Investigator Grant. A good three hours resulted in the refinement of the significance section and initiation of the writing of the method section.

Sunday, March 15. I always like to spend Sunday evening planning for my week's activities as well as making final adjustment to my plan for Tuesday's class. The class consists of one hour of clinical conference and two hours of seminar. I xeroxed an interesting article for discussion at the clinical conference on how nurses charged for their care on a labor and delivery unit. Notes were made to ask specific students to present what they had written about in their logs so that the other students could discuss the care and make suggestions for improvement. Since I had already developed an outline for the class on support groups, I spent about 1-1/2 hours reading additional articles that I had found. I also reviewed an article I had co-authored on Infertility support groups so that I would have the specifics at my finger tips.

Faculty Member's Summary Observations. Keeping a seven-day "diary" has been an enlightening experience for me. It is clear that I spend many more hours working than I believe the public would guess. Whereas the role of the professor is often divided into teaching, research and service, the boundaries become less obvious with my descriptions of activities I am engaged in. My teaching is greatly enhanced by the service and research that I perform.

It is now clear to me that a written log provides a contextual understanding of the faculty's activities, which results in a much better way of assessing workload than merely using time spent. Completion of the written log takes considerable effort and time. However, a several-day investment of time on an annual basis hardly seems overwhelming. The log's worth is well recognized if it is used by administrators in decisions about future workload and productivity as well as in evaluation of faculty performance.

Results from the Workload Study. For all six units participating in the faculty workload study, the three parts of the study (faculty productivity worksheets, the single-page numerical survey, and the weekly logs) were consistent in what they demonstrated. Specifically, faculty worked about 52 hours on the average during the sample week. Although the types of instructional activities varied widely among the six units, on the average faculty in five of the six units spent about 54 percent of their time on instruction-related activities. The exception was the Salem Regional Campus, where about 64 percent of faculty time was devoted to instruction-related activities. The percent of an average work week spent on research and creative activities varied from 25 to 35 percent. Faculty in the six units spent approximately 14 percent of the average work week in service activities, including administrative duties and professional and public service. Results of the pilot faculty workload study indicate that using the academic department or school as the unit of analysis yields a far more accurate picture of overall faculty productivity than workload analyses that focus on individual faculty. As an effective and valid unit of analysis, the department or school help convey the breadth and complexity of faculty activities. These observations make it tempting to conclude that in contrast to some of the rhetoric at the national level and from state governments, Kent faculty in the surveyed units are not only working hard, they are actually working hard on the right tasks.

If it is assumed that faculty workload profiles at peer institutions are compatible with those of faculty at Kent State University, then an interesting question arises. Is the issue of whether faculty are spending too much time in research and too little time in instruction-related activities a dominant issue for all major universities, or is it an issue that is mostly confined to and in need of more attention at the Carnegie Research I universities? This question becomes most relevant if national and state debates on workload and time devoted to instruction-related activities paint all major universities with the same brush.

Departmental Productivity. The faculty workload study suggests the need for flexibility to optimize the strengths of individual faculty. In the context of flexible workloads, however, it is appropriate for universities to have some type of overall department workload and productivity expectations. In this spirit, Kent State University is experimenting with another type of workload study that projects unit level productivity expectations from a student–faculty ratio point of view.

The student–faculty ratio approach establishes unit-specific ratios of full-time equated students (FTES) to full-time equated faculty (FTEF). The provost's office at Kent has developed expected (assigned) student–faculty ratios by unit and level of instruction. Expected ratios generally are smaller for upper-division and graduate classes than for lower-division and undergraduate classes and depend on the academic discipline. How do the ratios tie to faculty workload? The number of students in classes is clearly an ingredient of faculty and unit workload. Student–faculty ratios assume on the average that faculty teach not only assigned classes, but also that those classes are sufficiently enrolled. Thus they can be considered one important parameter in determining overall department workload and productivity.

To illustrate, assume a large, Ph.D.-granting humanities department at Kent has a total of 74.8 budgeted FTEF (full-time faculty, part-time faculty, and graduate assistants equated to FTEF). It offers four levels of courses and instruction: general studies (GS), baccalaureate (BAC), master's (MAS), and doctoral (DOC). Assigned student–faculty ratios (FTES/FTEF) for the department by instructional levels are GS, 22/1; BAC, 18/1; MAS, 15/1; and DOC, 10/1. In a given academic year, this large humanities department had full-time equated students by instructional levels as follows: GS, 844.4 FTES; BAC, 520 FTES; MAS, 32.4 FTES; and DOC, 37.2 FTES. Thus, the total for the academic year was 1434.4 FTES. The actual student–faculty ratio for this department was then Total FTES/Actual FTEF = 1434.4/74.8 = 19.2/1.

How does this actual student–faculty ratio compare with the expected workload student–faculty ratio? The answer to this question requires calculations involving the assigned student–faculty ratios by levels. Because the assigned student–faculty ratio at the GS level is 22/1 and 844.4 FTES were generated at the GS level, productivity at this level would project a need for 844.4/22 = 38.4 FTEF. Similarly, productivity at the BAC level would project a need for 520/18 = 28.8 FTEF; productivity at the MAS level would project a need for 32.4/15 = 2.2 FTEF; and productivity at the DOC level would project a need for 37.2/10 = 3.7 FTEF. Thus, based on actual full-time equated students generated, the assigned ratios by levels of instruction would predict a need for 38.4 + 28.8 + 2.2 + 3.7 = 73.2 FTEF. The expected overall student–faculty ratio for this department is then 1434.4 FTES/73.2 FTEF = 19.6/1. This expected student–faculty ratio of 19.6/1 compares with the actual student–faculty ratio of 19.2/1, and the expected or generated number of full-time equated faculty is 73.2 compared with an actual number of full-time equated faculty of 74.8. Thus, this department's actual productivity in a student–faculty ratio sense is very close to its expected productivity in a student–faculty ratio sense.

Because student–faculty ratios as workload and productivity measures at Kent are unit focused and not applied to particular classes or individuals, the humanities department has the latitude to schedule some small-enrollment classes and can vary teaching assignments in appropriate ways as long as the overall expected student–faculty ratio is realized.

As noted earlier, expected student–faculty ratios will differ among units. For example, the School of Nursing at Kent State University has an assigned BAC ratio of 10/1 and an assigned MAS ratio of 8/1. Instruction in clinical settings and national accreditation requirements are largely responsible for these lower ratios.

Concluding Observations

Kent State University has conducted several studies involving faculty workload and productivity expectations during the last two years. Much of the effort converges on a basic theme: faculty workloads and productivity expectations at Kent are and should be varied, and varied fairly. The Faculty Senate Commission on Scholarship concluded in the spirit of Boyer's *Scholarship Reconsidered* that a variety of forms of rigorous scholarship at Kent are appropriate and rewardable. The Andresen study exhibited through the faculty productivity worksheets and faculty logs the rich breadth of scholarly activities, including teaching, that Kent faculty perform. This three-part study also provided valuable information not only about the total number of hours faculty spend in professional activities in an average week, but also the percentage of time spent in given categories of professional endeavors (based on the six-unit pilot workload study, faculty at the Kent Campus are spending about 54 percent of their professional time in instruction-related activities).

In terms of faculty workload and productivity expectations, the Kent Pew Roundtable principles, major strategic planning goals and objectives, and the Commission on Scholarship principles all stressed overall productivity for faculty in contrast to productivity of a prescribed kind for each faculty member. These approaches led naturally to another theme in the workload puzzle: unit productivity and how individual faculty contribute to the overall productivity of the unit. In terms of students served, expected student–faculty ratios by levels of instruction and academic discipline are an example of productivity in a unit sense.

Kent State University has made considerable progress in developing coherent and appropriate faculty and unit workload expectations, primarily through its own workload initiatives but also by recognizing workload efforts at state and national levels. The progress the university has enjoyed has depended on collaboration between faculty and administration. All the initiatives have involved substantial input from concerned parties. This is not to say that each individual has agreed with every decision on an expanded view of scholarship, the *Principles for the Evaluation and Reward of Faculty Scholarship*, assigned unit level student–faculty ratios, or the goals and objectives featured in the strategic plan. However, most faculty do acknowledge there have been opportunities to help shape outcomes. In the words of Kent's Pew Roundtable and strategic plan, perhaps the university is achieving an environment of shared decision making and shared accountability, and hence is cultivating a stakeholder-oriented strategy for continuous improvement. Further progress on workload issues will require continued cooperation, realistic expectations, and mutual respect among all parties in these challenging times for higher education.

Reference

Boyer, E. L. *Scholarship Reconsidered.* Princeton, N.J.: Carnegie Foundation for the Advancement of Teaching, 1990.

GREER GLAZER is professor of nursing at Kent State University and past chair of the faculty senate.

MYRON S. HENRY is provost and professor of mathematics at Kent State University.

*Recommendations and a rationale for the contents of a manage-
ment data base about an institution's human assets are presented.*

Information for Strategic Decision Making: The Faculty Data Base

Dennis P. Jones

Although colleges and universities fulfill a variety of functions, they all have in common the development of the talents of those who come to them as students. Furthermore, these institutions depend absolutely on the knowledge and skills of other individuals—the faculty and staff—to meet the educational needs of the students and to accomplish the other purposes of the institution. The centrality of people to the success of any college or university means that these people—students, faculty, and staff—must be recognized as the key assets of all institutions.

Despite the centrality of people as key institutional assets, many organizational cultures have resisted the notion that they are obligated to manage these assets, especially their faculty assets. They are much more comfortable dealing with personal needs, interests, and capabilities of individuals than with the more abstract issues of creating, maintaining, and appropriately using the collective human assets of the enterprise. However, the environment in which colleges and universities are now operating—and in which they will probably operate for years to come—makes it impossible to duck the broader issue. There is widespread recognition that institutions of postsecondary education have much to offer a wide variety of different clients. As Margaret Miller points out in Chapter One, demands placed on these institutions are increasing, and available resources are not keeping pace with this increase in demand. As a consequence, a widespread expectation is emerging among both administrators and institutional constituents that colleges and universities must, and will, find a way to do more with less.

In short, institutions must improve their productivity. This goal can be accomplished only if institutions find creative ways to enhance the productivity of their key assets, a fact recognized by institutional administrators and external constituents alike. Most academic administrators are fully aware that their people decisions are becoming more and more important and more and more difficult. They are under increasing pressure from legislators and other external constituents who are taking a keen interest in (and providing much of the impetus for) institutional efforts to improve their productivity. In some states, this interest has extended to statutory prescription of teaching loads. In the majority of states that have stopped short of such prescription, the expectation of improved productivity (and the ability to demonstrate that improvement) is nonetheless made clear in many ways. In this environment, administrators are struggling to respond to external needs and pressures without destroying institutional cultures and voiding social compacts between faculty and administrators that have been established over the years. It is a critical—and extraordinarily difficult—assignment.

This set of conditions has created new demands for data about faculty and staff, but especially about the faculty. These demands are being expressed by a variety of potential users. Institutional administrators are seeking information that will help them make critical decisions about staffing levels, compensation, and personnel assignments in an increasingly unforgiving environment. Researchers are seeking data that will help them better understand the conditions and consequences of changed faculty work patterns. External audiences are seeking evidence that their admonitions are being heard and that institutions are responding to the calls for productivity. The purpose of this chapter is to provide an overview of a tool—a new handbook—designed to help institutional researchers and other analysts provide the information these various audiences are legitimately seeking.

The development of this handbook was initiated when it became painfully clear that the data resources needed to respond to emerging information needs were sadly lacking in most institutions. In attempting to respond to these varying demands for data, the responsible staffs in most institutions have found their available data resources sadly lacking. In attempting to respond to internal requests, institutional researchers have discovered that faculty data bases have been created to serve the operational rather than the strategic decision-making needs of the institution. All institutions have an ongoing need to record the terms and conditions of employment, pay faculty members, administer the benefits to which faculty are entitled, assign them to teach classes and to other activities, and make decisions about salary increases, tenure, and promotion. These different operational functions are located in a variety of different units within the institution. Consequently, so are most of the supporting data. Faced with the necessity of pulling together data necessary to respond to the decision-making needs of institutional administrators, analysts find themselves dealing with incomplete data located in multiple files built around definitions and coding schemes that are often inconsistent. In the most extreme cases, even an individual's identification code varies across the different files. All too often, data compilation and analysis take longer than the decision context allows, and decision makers are left in the uncomfortable position of navigating their way through difficult choices without information that could help.

In dealing with the external world, the data provider's job is made even more complex by the absence of a language that has consistent meaning. For example, terms such as *effort, workload,* and *productivity* often are used interchangeably or are assigned different meanings by the participants in the discussion. Even when generally common meaning is assigned to a term, there remains the problem of quantifying the concept in a way that appropriately reflects the concept and is standardized so that all institutions responding to a legislative or other external data request are doing so in a similar fashion. Terms as commonly used as *salary* and *compensation* are made less comparable by different reporting periods (nine-month or eleven-month) and by the differences between base and actual.

Faced with increasing needs for faculty data and lacking guidance regarding the development of the requisite data base and the calculation of key derived variables, representatives of several higher education associations—the Association for Institutional Research (AIR), the Society for College and University Planning (SCUP), the Association for the Study of Higher Education (ASHE), the State Higher Education Executive Officers (SHEEO), and the American Education Research Association (AERA) Division J—came together to respond to this need. This effort led to a grant of seed money from the Teachers Insurance and Annuity Association (TIAA) and, subsequently, to allocation of development funds by the National Center for Education Statistics (NCES) for the development of a *Handbook on Human Assets* (Jones and Lovell, in press). The staff work associated with developing this document was contracted to the National Center for Higher Education Management Systems (NCHEMS). The final document should be available from NCES in late 1994 or early 1995.

The *Handbook* seeks to accomplish several purposes. In summary, those purposes are as follows:

Establish a solid conceptual framework for dealing with strategic issues regarding faculty and other employees of a college or university—a framework that distinguishes issues surrounding individuals and their characteristics from those pertaining to types, quantities, and uses of the human assets available to an institution.

Identify the data elements required as the contents of an analytic data base designed to support both decision making about faculty and staff within the institution and necessary external reporting.

Define these data elements and specify subcategorization and coding schemes where appropriate.

Prepare definitions for important derived data elements—workload and productivity that are not recorded directly but are the result of calculations involving other elements—and the conventions by which quantitative values for these terms might be calculated.

Suggest "good practice" in the use of these data for internal decision making, for exchange among institutions, and for reporting basic descriptive data to state and federal agencies.

This is an ambitious undertaking and only time will tell whether the *Handbook* achieves its objectives. In this brief chapter, I make no attempt to summarize the extensive contents of that document. Rather, I provide an overview of the important underlying concepts surrounding the design and intended uses of the suggested data base.

The Basic Concepts

The *Handbook* is based on the premise that in order to effectively address issues about faculty at the strategic level, it is useful to recognize faculty not only as individuals but as key institutional assets. Numerous institutionwide issues—not the least of which are issues of diversity—require the ability to collect and summarize data about individual faculty and staff members. An even greater variety of issues revolve around the concept of faculty and staff as key institutional assets, questions about choices associated with the creation and maintenance of the asset, about quantity and quality of the available asset, about the cost of the asset, about its allocation and use, and about the consequences of this allocation of resources in terms of outputs achieved. In some cases, it is important to know information for which the individual is the appropriate unit of analysis. Other cases call for information about the FTE faculty. Each of these components of decision making about the human assets of an institution is discussed briefly in this section. All are discussed in considerably more detail in the *Handbook*.

Faculty as Individuals. As noted earlier, one of the features considered most desirable in a college or university is an ability to deal on a personal level with individuals who voluntarily join the campus community as students, faculty, or staff. Most institutions do very well at this level. Indeed, they often focus so much attention on the day-to-day needs of the individual that they ignore some of the strategic issues associated with the faculty as a collective. For example, most institutions are acutely aware of the importance of compiling data about the diversity of the campus community as measured in terms of the racial and gender composition of the faculty and staff. Depending on the nature of the institution and the characteristics of the students, it may be equally important to compile other data that describe the faculty as a whole. For example, it may be important to know the proportion of faculty who have experienced similar institutional settings as students or employees at other colleges. (It is hard to sustain the culture and values of a community college or a liberal arts college if the overwhelming experience of the collective faculty has been in major research universities.) Similarly, it may be important to know the breadth and depth of foreign language proficiency of the faculty, especially if the institution is attracting increasing numbers of students from other countries.

The Notion of Human Assets. Although the importance of data about the unique capacities and interests of faculty members as individuals almost goes without saying, for planning and management purposes it is more important to monitor the characteristics and capabilities of the faculty as a whole than to be concerned about the background and abilities of any one individual. When considering data needed for strategic decision-making purposes, it may be more important to invoke the metaphor of faculty as human assets. Such a view has the potential to lead institutional administrators to consider their decisions about faculty in a somewhat different light. For example, it leads to a recognition that acquisition of new full-time faculty is better viewed as an investment decision than as a purchase. Along the same lines, it heightens the distinction between hiring a full-time faculty member (an investment decision) and contracting with part-time faculty (a purchase of services). Finally, and perhaps most importantly, the concept of faculty as a human asset helps draw attention to the need for ongoing expenditure on professional development for faculty members. Assets need continued attention if they are not to lose their value to the institution with the passage of time. Buildings deteriorate over time and most library books lose their currency. Without opportunities for professional rejuvenation through research or other professional development activity, the faculty can also become outdated. In times of particularly constrained resources, it is easy to forget the importance of reinvestment in human assets: sabbaticals, travel to professional meetings, and other professional development activities are often among the first items reduced or eliminated when budgets get tight.

The *Handbook* discusses this concept more fully and suggests ways in which information can be used to help institutional administrators understand the consequences, particularly financial, of decisions to invest in new human assets and to track the level of institutional commitment to the maintenance of those assets.

Type of Human Asset. Colleges and universities are complex organizations requiring employees with widely varying skills and abilities. Most institutions have extensive classification systems that distinguish employees with different types and levels of responsibilities, abilities, and experience. For example, it is common for such systems to have numerous categories of clerical staff, ranging from entry-level typist to executive secretary. For purposes of supporting both internal decision making and external communication, such classification schemes disguise at least as much as they reveal. Institutional executives need a far simpler classification scheme for most of the broad, institutional issues they address. In recognition of the need for a more aggregate and generic set of categories, the *Handbook* reaffirms the appropriateness of the general schema being used by NCES, specifically the following:

Exempt Employees
Executive/administrative/managerial professionals
Instruction/research professionals (a more generic and specific category that includes most individuals commonly called faculty)
Specialists/support professionals
Nonexempt Employees
Technical employees
Office/clerical employees
Crafts/trades employees
Service employees

Quantity and Quality of Assets Available. As with any asset, an understanding of the amount of human assets available to the institution is basic to managerial effectiveness. A straightforward count of number of employees of various types is seldom a sufficient measure because many institutional employees work less than full-time. The tradition has been to use full-time equivalents (FTEs) as the measure of asset availability. Recognizing the definitional variations associated with this particular measure, the *Handbook* suggests use of the service-month as an alternative measure of asset availability (where a service-month is full-time availability for one month). This is a slightly more precise measure than FTE but less difficult to obtain than more detailed measures such as service-days.

Whereas measurement of asset quantity is relatively straightforward, assessment of quality is much more difficult. When such evaluation is done, through processes used to determine merit-based pay increases or through other formal evaluation procedures, the unit of analysis is almost invariably the individual faculty or staff member. Administrators seldom see data that would help them evaluate the quality of the faculty as a whole and to identify particularly weak spots, yet it is just such data that are central to discussions about where to invest scarce resources in faculty development. The *Handbook* recognizes both the importance of dealing with the concept of quality and the practical difficulties of doing so.

Information about the quantity and quality of all types of employees is ultimately important to institutional leaders. However, the expense and critical importance of faculty to the effectiveness of the institution invariably focuses disproportionate attention on this particular category of employee.

Cost of the Asset. Data to aid in decision making about faculty compensation are readily available in most institutions. Consideration of faculty as assets leads to the need for additional kinds of cost data that are much less readily available at most institutions. The first of these costs is the acquisition cost, the costs associated with paying for laboratory equipment, moving expenses, reduced teaching loads, graduate assistants, and other inducements offered to attract a faculty member to the campus. The other cost component is the cost associated with the maintenance—the continuing professional development—

of the human asset. Both are key considerations in the context of planning and budgeting decisions. The *Handbook* recommends compiling data on the full array of costs incurred when a faculty member or senior administrator is hired and on the allocation of institutional effort (time and money) to professional development.

Allocation and Use of the Available Human Assets. Data about types, amounts, quality, and costs of an institution's human assets are essential ingredients in decisions that focus on the acquisition and maintenance of those assets. There is another class of strategic decisions of equal or greater importance—decisions regarding how available assets will be assigned to organizational units and functions within the institution. Faculty members almost always have the ability to perform more than one function; they can teach classes, perform scholarly activities, advise and counsel students, provide professional expertise to aid practitioners in their field, and perform certain administrative duties for the institution. Other types of employees can also be flexible resources (for example, some administrators can teach). These examples reinforce the point that the most flexible resource available to an institution is the time and attention of its human asset, and that the allocation of this resource is the key to achieving institutional priorities. Information that provides an overview of how the human assets of the institution are being (and have been) allocated is essential to informed institutional decision making. The *Handbook* recommends means by which data about the allocation of different types of human assets to various institutional functions can be compiled and displayed.

Effort, Workload, Output, and Productivity. Finally, a set of managerial and external communication issues depend on data about the consequences of the allocation and use of the human assets of the institution. What did we achieve with this particular investment of human talent and energy? At this point, language and a focus on only the instruction function get in the way of communication between educational administrators and important external constituents. The language problems exist primarily around the terms *effort, workload, output,* and *productivity*. To address this problem, the *Handbook* suggests the following conventions:

Effort: the amount of time expressed in FTEs or, preferably, service-months allocated to (or used in) a particular function (such as instruction or research).

Workload: the sum (within a particular category) of the discrete measures of responsibility assigned: x faculty contact hours of classroom instruction, y thesis students directed, z research projects directed. Workload is a measure of activity.

Output: the consequences or products resulting from the tasks performed, such as student credit hours produced, research papers and other scholarly works prepared, and research grants prepared and submitted. The term *outputs* is used explicitly to separate this concept from *outcomes,* which is normally taken to mean such things as students' gain in knowledge and skills and new knowledge created.

Productivity: outputs produced per unit of effort, such as student credit hours produced per FTE instructional faculty and research papers produced per FTE research faculty.

These are the terms in which external accountability questions are invariably raised. This reality, if no other, makes them measures that should be viewed critically by institutional administrators. Experience indicates, however, that these measures are infrequently applied at aggregate units of analysis. Rather, they are viewed in the context of the individual faculty member. Such a focus is appropriate when the focus of the decision is on the individual—merit pay, promotion, or tenure decisions. However, strategic decision making requires that the focus be shifted to major units or the institution as a whole. Institutional decision makers (and, in some cases, external bodies) may want to enhance the productivity of the institution or its major components. In all cases, however, the department or unit head and the affected faculty should be left with the decision about assignments (and therefore productivity) of individual faculty members.

Interrelationship of Concepts. Figure 5.1 summarizes some of the key relationships addressed in the *Handbook*. It reflects data about individuals as the starting point, then indicates the necessity of shifting the focus from individuals to assets of different kinds that are allocated to various functions within the institution. Finally, it indicates the need for systematic attention to linkages between the allocation of personnel effort and the consequence of that allocation.

Strategic decision making and external communication revolve around the set of concepts and issues presented in this section. An overview of an analytic data base designed to provide the analyst with the data needed to address these issues is presented in the following section.

The Basic Data Structure

As noted previously, data about faculty and other institutional employees tend to be scattered in numerous files (electronic and paper) throughout the institution. Although the data may be scattered, experience indicates that most of the data needed to support strategic decision making are, in fact, available somewhere within most institutions. The requirement, therefore, is to get the data organized in a manner useful to the analyst. There is little sense in seeking to replace or combine the numerous operating systems designed to meet the ongoing needs of various offices on the campus. Rather, the objective should be to create a receptacle—a management data base—into which selected data from various sources can be placed for use by the analysts charged with providing information to support decision making and external communication.

Figure 5.1. Interrelationship of Concepts

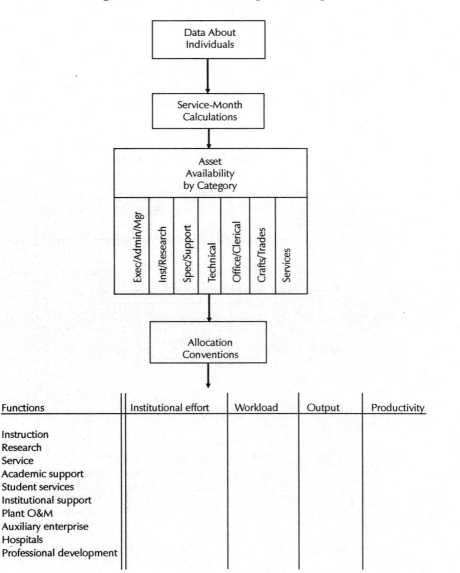

The data structure suggested for this purpose is modeled generally after the structure of a student tracking system—a basic set of descriptive data for each employee that will change little, if at all; a set of annual and term data that capture employment conditions, assignments, workload, and outputs; and a set of data about conditions of the employees' separation from the institution. The following outline presents the major features of a suggested data base. The reader is referred to the *Handbook* for details. Suggestions for specific data elements are included in that document, along with definitions, subcategorization, and coding schemes for these elements.

Outline of a Management Data Base about Faculty and Other Employees

A. Identifier and Demographic Descriptors
   1. Descriptors such as date of birth, race, gender, citizenship, and disability status
   2. Foreign language proficiency and other skill and interest indicators
B. Academic History
   1. Level, field, date, and granting institutions for all academic degrees
   2. Data about professional licenses
C. Employment History at Institution
   1. Recruitment activity—the acquisition cost
   2. Initial employment status
   3. Major decision points such as tenure and promotion
   4. Most recent professional development activity
D. Current Year Employment Conditions
   1. Contract terms—rank or title, term of appointment, competition
   2. EEOC classification and service months
E. Assignments/Workload
   1. Allocation of effort to functions
   2. Workloads (classes taught, research projects directed)
      (Note: It may be appropriate to have two blocks of assignment and workload data, one at the beginning of the term and another at the end.)
F. Outputs
   1. Products and services produced
   2. Performance evaluations—qualitative judgments
G. Separation
   1. Date and type of separation
   2. Information about subsequent employment

Such a data base allows the analyst to do both longitudinal and cross-sectional analyses and to address the typical strategic issues regarding faculty faced by most colleges and universities.

Uses of These Data. The management data base described above has been designed to support an array of strategic decisions that *should be* at the forefront of concern internally to most institutions—decisions that focus on creating a human asset pool that is appropriate in size and capability to the needs of the institution, allocating and using that pool in such a way that institutional priorities are achieved, and taking steps to ensure that professional development opportunities are provided commensurate with the need to keep faculty and staff current in their fields and capable of superior contributions to the institution.

Specific analyses that could be performed using the suggested data base are far too numerous to list here. Following are some illustrations:

Profiles of institutional employees according to demographic and academic preparation characteristics

Faculty flows—likely retirements and new hiring requirements

Trends in amounts of human assets of various kinds available to the institution

Allocation of human assets to organizational units and functions

Price and cost analyses: acquisition costs, average salaries and wages, leave liabilities and extra or overtime compensation

Workload, output, and productivity measures for the institution as a whole and its subunits

Level of investment in personal and professional development

Such analyses should cover most of the analytic agenda for most institutions.

Other Uses. Although the primary uses of the data base are to support institutional decision making, it has been designed to produce data for other purposes as well. The first of these uses is the interinstitutional exchange of data. Because so few absolute standards exist regarding how best to allocate resources to institutional functions, it has become common for institutional administrators to seek insights by comparing conditions in their institution with those at similar institutions. Such comparisons are particularly common when looking at expenditures of financial resources across various institutional functions. The *Handbook* specifically recognizes this requirement and suggests "good practice" in exchanging data on such topics as average salaries, salaries of new faculty, and allocation of human assets to institutional functions.

The kinds of data often sought through interinstitutional exchange are also often sought by agencies of state and federal government. This use, too, has been recognized in the *Handbook* with procedures and formats suggested for the most common types of reporting requirements.

Finally are the uses associated with communicating information—for example, workload, output, and productivity—to external audiences. Some jurisdictions have a considerable history of reporting productivity data for the instruction function (such as student credit hours per FTE faculty) to state agencies, the legislature, and other bodies. This limited focus ignores the broader missions of some institutions and can put these more complex institutions at a severe disadvantage, especially when primary attention is given to measures of instructional workload rather than measures of productivity. The *Handbook* addresses these issues and suggests good practice, but is by no means the final word on this topic. It lays out a sound conceptual framework and puts the relevant pieces in context. However, because certain measures (particularly those for the outputs of functions other than instruction) have not been widely accepted as conventions, the *Handbook* attempts to move institutions toward more clear, precise, and comparable analyses of faculty information rather than serve as the final authority in this domain.

Problems and Pitfalls. The problems facing the analyst attempting to create and use a management data base dealing with issues of faculty and other employees will be of two quite different kinds. First will be a series of technical problems associated with trying to compile a reasonable set of data from existing sources. The critical problems will deal with definitions, periodicity, and extraction of data from nonelectronic sources. Because so few institutions have a data architecture (categories and codes) that is strictly enforced across administrative record systems, it is extremely likely that early attempts to compile data from different sources will reveal all manner of definitional and coding problems. Every experienced institutional researcher has experienced this problem, but through persistent attention to details it can be overcome.

Periodicity of data will be another problem: what is needed for a full year will be available only for one or two terms; what is desired at the beginning of the term will be available only at the end of the term; and so forth. In this circumstance there is little choice but to make do with what's available and try to negotiate changes with the operational data users a step at a time.

Finally is the problem associated with creating a data base from hard-copy reports. At many colleges and universities, certain key records—about use, outputs, and workload, for example—take the form of individual faculty reports that are kept in individual faculty file folders in the office of the dean or academic vice president. Gaining access to such records and devising schema that allow these basic descriptive data to be recorded in a data base in an appropriate way is, and will probably remain, a major challenge to most analysts, and will probably require the active involvement of the chief academic officer of the institution.

The political issues are clear and, for many institutions, legitimately threatening. Most institutions have had little experience in using institutionwide data on faculty workload and productivity for internal purposes, particularly as those measures extend beyond the instruction function. As a result, they have little real feel for the data and what they will reveal about their institution. With external pressure for such information mounting, and with enough data being provided in enough places to prove that it can be done, it is increasingly difficult to plead inability to provide. The initial objectives, then, must be to level the definitional and procedural playing field and argue for a focus on produc- tivity rather than workload on the premise that the institution should be held responsible for the result, not directed at how to achieve it. Even if these objectives are met, however, some institutions will be embarrassed by the revelations of such data. Failure to address productivity problems as an internal, strategic issue rather than as a communications problem will inevitably cause heartburn in some quarters. There are probably some quarters where tough questions from external audiences will, in the long term, serve the institution well. In the short run, however, it will not be a fun experience for those closest to the action and to the numbers.

Reference

Jones, D., and Lovell, C. *Handbook on Human Assets: Record-Keeping and Analysis* (Technical Review Draft). Boulder, Colo.: National Center for Higher Education Management Systems (NCHEMS), in press.

DENNIS P. JONES *is president of the National Center for Higher Education Management Systems (NCHEMS) in Boulder, Colorado.*

Examples of how to define, collect, and report data on faculty workload are provided from published reports of various institutions.

Practical Considerations and Suggestions for Measuring Faculty Workload

Lloyd Byrd, Jr.

Public sentiment is growing that colleges and universities should be getting more productivity from their resources and should be more accountable to those who provide those resources (Heydinger and Simsek, 1992). As Dennis Jones observed in Chapter Five, colleges' and universities' survival depends on the knowledge and skills of their faculty and staff. For an institution to assess how well it is meeting the goals and objectives of its missions, it must be able to define and measure what its faculty produce. Based on experience with the issues and the data associated with faculty workload measurement, institutional research (IR) offices are normally well-positioned to support the development and implementation of faculty workload measurement, analysis, and reporting.

In this chapter, I first review course load analysis, the traditional method used to define, measure, and report faculty workload. I then suggest some alternatives for collecting other types of data on faculty workload and related issues to be considered as IR offices try to meet emerging institutional needs for information on evaluation and accountability. By the end of this chapter, readers should be able to search out existing workload data within their institutions, compile a simple course load data base, and be able to recommend methods for collecting workload data to meet their institutions' future needs.

Faculty Course Load Analysis

Measurement of faculty course loads is probably the most basic and popular method currently used to quantify faculty workload. Recently, measurement of course loads has become much more important. As Margaret Miller notes in Chapter One, Virginia is one of several states that has seen a rise in public and legislative interest in faculty teaching loads at public colleges and universities. Two examples of this rise in interest are a week-long series of articles coordinated among Virginia newspapers in September 1993 that featured examples of light faculty course loads, and recent legislation (introduced but not acted on in Virginia) to mandate minimum faculty instructional contact hours ("A College Education at What Cost?," 1993).

The first step in preparing a course load analysis is to define what it is intended to provide. Although this step may seem obvious, it is an essential one that must be done at the beginning. Various administrators will have different expectations about what a data base will do for them. The IR office must quantify those expectations and review them with appropriate administrators to be sure the correct types of data are collected and reported.

Often, efforts to measure course loads will be tailored to specific purposes, such as a review of resource allocations or an evaluation of unit performance. As a result, data are not always comparable across reports. For example, one year's report may focus on all faculty for a single semester, whereas the next may focus only on full-time faculty for a whole academic year. A reporting format with a reasonable amount of detail on faculty types (full-time versus adjunct), course measures (headcounts, credit hours, and sections), and meeting times and places should be developed and used regularly so comparable data accumulate across years.

Collecting Course Load Data at VCU. The institutional research office at Virginia Commonwealth University (VCU) has conducted a number of analyses of faculty course loads during recent years. The generic process to collect course load data is outlined below and should provide an adequate starting point for similar course load analyses on other campuses.

Collect Enrollment Data. The process starts by extracting data from the university's student information system (SIS). In our experience, semester-end data have the most complete record of critical information such as class enrollments and assigned instructor(s). Enrollment information is kept on individual students but in too much detail for faculty course load analyses. Data on individual students must be combined into a single record for each section (including labs and independent studies) that summarizes the information about the section. At a minimum, each section record should contain fields that identify the following information: the department offering the course, the course and section number (as the key to the record), course credit hours, the year and term of the record, total student credit hours and headcounts, section meeting times and places, names and social security numbers (SSNs) of the instructors, and any special course designators that identify laboratory, off-campus, or other special sections.

Collect Faculty Data. The second step is to extract faculty data from the institution's human resource system. This step is important for two reasons.

First, the human resource system has data on all faculty employed by the institution, where the SIS typically has data only on faculty who are currently assigned to teach. The human resource data base provides independent enumeration of the total pool of faculty resources (which should include full-time faculty, adjunct or part-time faculty, and graduate assistants). An independent source of faculty data is very important if the goal of the course load analysis is a calculation of overall departmental cost effectiveness or a comparison of actual course loads with the department's course offering capacity. Second, the human resource system has information about faculty members, such as their employee status, salary, special funding, academic rank, and tenure status, that is not available in the SIS.

Merge the Enrollment and Faculty Data. The third step is to merge the personnel and SIS data into a course load data base. The instructor's SSN is the key for matching course and faculty data. Names are used to match records that do not share a common SSN (often due to transposed digits). The merger produces a course load data base that contains one record for every section in the institution, plus a record for every faculty member who has no current teaching assignment.

Review the Data Base Contents. The final step in the process is to review and clean up the data base. Here are some basic problems to watch for. First, look for sections with no student headcounts. Generally, these records should be dropped. Similarly, look for sections without a valid instructor of record (Dr. Staff can be a very busy person in some units). Accurate faculty data should be added to the data base for these sections. Also look for multiple records that represent only part of a single section. For example, a single large lecture section in math or computer science may actually appear as 10 to 15 small breakout sections in the SIS data base. Combining breakout section records is not necessary for analyses of student credit hours or headcounts but must be done for reports on section loads. These breakout sections can often be identified (and section counts corrected) because they are listed as being taught by the same instructor on the same days and times and in the same room. Finally, sections that represent one–to–one student interactions with faculty should be identified. These independent study or student research listings should not be mixed with regular courses in an analysis of section loads because the effort associated with them is typically less than that needed for regular sections. Because they do represent instructional effort, they should be reported in some format.

Once all the changes are made, review the data base with the academic units who offer the courses. They will have insight into things that may look peculiar, provide additional missing data, and generally will be interested in what you are doing and how they can help to make the process better in the future.

Course Load Studies at Other Schools. There are many variations on this basic process described above. The three examples below represent the basic process and offer some unique ideas to be considered.

Despite its age, a report published by Colorado State University presents solid descriptions of the issues surrounding the need for faculty workload measurements and provides some interesting ideas for comparative measurement and evaluation of faculty instructional workloads (Colorado State University, 1975). Colorado State's intent was to measure direct instructional, related instructional, and related professional activities of full-time instructional faculty members. The beginning section of the report provides an excellent summary of the three traditional methods used to quantify instructional workload (course credit hours taught, student FTEs taught, and student credit hours taught) and their weaknesses in describing instructional workloads.

Colorado State devised a concept called the Comparative Staffing Unit (CSU) to summarize instructional workload. The CSU was a weighted scale designed to measure the professional input necessary to carry out specific activities. An average workload for a year was set at 1,000 CSUs, based on an average 50–hour work week. For direct instruction, the effort associated with one course credit hour of lecture became the standard unit of measure for all instructional activities. Detailed calculations and examples of actual workload transformations are presented at the end of the report, along with a flow chart of the data sources used for the workload analysis.

Shull (1984) describes the point-based system that measures faculty course load in the division of science, engineering, and technology at Penn State's Behrend College. The main assumption of this system is that instructional workload consists of three elements: classroom contact time, grading and evaluation time, and laboratory and practicum time. The system applies points to course assignments (not the courses themselves), making adjustments for repeated sections, large enrollments, and team-teaching assignments. Actual workloads are compared with a calculated standard workload called a consensus full-time load, which is based on the typical expected workload for a full-time math faculty member. A series of formulas are used to calculate the workload measures for each of the three components outlined above. The process is automated using data from the student information system. The system produces periodic data bases and provides reports that show detailed workload components for each faculty member.

Hopper (1992) describes faculty workload measurement at Northern Arizona University (NAU) in a paper delivered at the 32nd Annual Forum of the Association for Institutional Research. Faculty workload is divided into three major components: direct instruction, indirect instruction, and noninstructional activities. The noninstructional component is based on the percent of annual FTE allocated to activities such as administration, service, and organized and sponsored research effort. No hard data comparable to course loads are collected for this component. The report provides a good technical description of processes used to extract data from the university student information system and personnel system and to generate reports for review by the department chairs. All of the information is incorporated into a faculty FTE database each semester. The data bases allow the IR office to address a number of both regular and special issues, including the impact of faculty release time, teaching loads of new versus continuing faculty, and average section counts and contact hours per faculty rank.

Faculty Workload Surveys

The faculty course load studies described above analyze data on only one aspect of faculty workload—instruction—from central student information system and human resource system records. In order to measure the other major workload components, scholarship and service, other sources of data must be found. Unfortunately, data bases on scholarship or service activities, as well as nonteaching instructional activities, rarely exist in most institutions.

As Stecklein (1961) notes, beyond central course load data, "it is necessary to use some type of report or survey form to collect information about the various activities that faculty perform" (p. 6). Surveys have been used by many institutions to document, from responses given by a representative sample, how faculty spread their effort across the entire workload spectrum. Stecklein also notes the importance of faculty participation and cooperation in the development of any data collection process. Finally, any data collection effort should have a clearly defined purpose and that purpose should be communicated to the faculty, especially if the process is intended to be an ongoing effort.

Survey of Virginia Faculty. A survey to document how faculty at Virginia's public colleges and universities actually used their professional time, how they would prefer to use their time, and their reactions to state budget reductions was conducted during the spring of 1991 by the State Council of Higher Education for Virginia (SCHEV). The survey process is typical of workload surveys reported in the literature and will demonstrate the strengths and weaknesses of faculty workload surveys.

The Virginia survey asked faculty to describe the number of hours in an average work week and the allocation of their effort across teaching, scholarship and service activities. The results showed Virginia faculty had an average work week of 52 hours and spent 55 percent of that time on teaching (a figure very close to that reported by Glazer and Henry in Chapter Four). Virginia faculty reported spending 26 percent of their time on scholarship and 19 percent on university and community service. The Virginia data are comparable to national data that showed teaching accounted for 56 percent of faculty effort at all public institutions, 43 percent at research universities, 47 percent at doctoral universities, and 62 percent at comprehensive institutions (Jordan and Layzell, 1992).

Surveys can also collect data on specific activities within major workload categories of teaching, research, and service. The Virginia survey divided instruction into eight subcategories (such as classroom, advising, and preparation time). Results showed that faculty from different types of institutions allocated their time differently, with community college faculty reporting more classroom contact time than faculty from other kinds of institutions.

Survey Strengths and Weaknesses.   Surveys can be cost–effective ways to collect data on faculty workload. Probability samples can provide good estimates of faculty workloads if they are drawn correctly, are combined with a reliable questionnaire, and do not have a large proportion of nonrespondents. The Virginia survey data proved very useful to VCU when a series of newspaper stories critical of Virginia's public colleges and universities was released ("A College Education at What Cost?," 1993). VCU had chosen to have enough of its faculty sampled within the Virginia survey to be able to make reliable estimates of faculty workloads for the institution. Access to this survey data allowed the IR office to quickly provide analyses that demonstrated that a great deal of behind the scenes work goes on for a single hour of classroom contact and that VCU faculty were engaged in a wide array of other professional activities.

On the downside, workload surveys depend on self-reported data. As this term implies, the data are provided directly by the faculty themselves. In contrast to centrally collected course load data, the survey data are generally perceived as subjective and can be treated with some skepticism by the public and by legislative organizations. Despite the shortcoming of self-reported data, it may be the only practical source of data on noninstructional faculty workloads.

Faculty Data Base

As the survey results from the previous section and other chapters in this volume demonstrate, faculty workload is composed of numerous factors. Most surveys report only how faculty allocate their effort, not what was actually produced by that effort. One of the biggest problems with measuring faculty workload is collecting, coding, and accessing data that quantifies scholarship and service activities. At present, there are no national standards for defining or reporting faculty workload measures. The *Handbook on Human Assets,* described in Chapter Five of this volume, begins to offer a solution to this problem, at least for reporting at the institutional level. Within an institution, one way to collect noninstructional data is to create a faculty data base. This effort represents the next logical step in workload data collection and analyses beyond course–load analyses.

The objective of a faculty data base is a central repository of quantitative data on the various scholarly and service efforts and products of the faculty. It should contain information on the major aspects of scholarship and service, such as publications, artistic performances, committee assignments, research grants and contracts, and professional awards and offices, for all faculty. These data can be merged with course load data for a more complete picture of faculty effort. The data base should be updated regularly without creating a significant data collection or reporting burden on the faculty or their departments.

Access to information about faculty by other faculty, students, and the public can also be an important reason for the development of an academic data base. The University of Maine System's academic data base, called UMSserve, is an example of a such a public service data base. UMSserve is "a single, system wide computerized database of public service resources" (University of Maine, 1993, p. 1). The system is supported by the university's library catalogue system, which allows easy access and retrieval of information.

The contents of the data base must be carefully considered and defined to ensure that consistent, useful data are collected. Specification of the variables in the data base operationalizes the major conceptual components of faculty effort. Establishing a relatively small set of variables that describes the efforts of all faculty is one of the most difficult tasks in developing an academic data base. Yuker (1984) recommends seven broad workload categories, described in Table 6.1. These definitions are consistent with the measurement data base Jones presents in Chapter Five of this volume.

Measuring research productivity is one of the most important and difficult parts of building the data base. Although the purpose of their chapter is to describe measurement of research productivity for faculty evaluation, much

Table 6.1. Basic Faculty Workload Categories

Basic Category	Subcategory Examples
Instruction	Time in class, preparation, evaluation, other student contact time
Research (can be divided into sponsored and departmental)	Writing books, articles, plays, or poems, preparing applications, experiments, and literature reviews
Professional development	Attending professional meetings, reviewing discipline-related materials, editing journals
Advisement and counseling	Student/career advising
Institutional service	Departmental and student record keeping, noninstructional committees
Public service	Unpaid consulting, lectures, and speeches related to expertise as a faculty member
Personal activities	Nonwork time spent on campus

Source: Data from Yuker, 1984, pp. 36–37.

of the discussion presented by Braxton and Bayer (1986) can be applied to the concept of measuring faculty workload. They note that "despite the ambiguity of citation practices, considerable evidence exists that citation counts provide an objective measure of productivity, significance, quality, utility, influence, effectiveness, or impact of a scholar" (Braxton and Bayer, 1986, pp. 34–35). The method does have limitations that must be kept in mind, such as establishing baseline counts, construction of citation indices, self-citation problems, the pool of potential citations, and the lack of citation coverage in some disciplines.

As Jones notes in Chapter Five of this volume, much of the data on faculty workload already exists electronically within the institution. For example, institutions routinely create data bases of grant proposals and awards, and departments create and maintain faculty vitae and annual reports on word processors. Though a very time consuming task, collecting such data is largely a matter of standardizing the format and putting it in a single location. Once collected, it must be accessible, and the tools for accessing an institutional data base can be categorized into three basic groups: personnel and human resource system components, Gopher data bases, and library catalogue data bases. Each of these options has strengths and weaknesses that should be weighed against the computer resources of the institution and the level of public access planned for the data base. A fourth option, a proprietary data service such as *Best North America*, described recently in the *Chronicle of Higher Education*, may be a viable option for some institutions ("New Data Base . . .," 1993, pp. 19–20).

Comprehensive Faculty Workload System

The final option for faculty workload analyses to be considered in this chapter is the comprehensive faculty workload system. Such a system quantifies all factors of faculty workload and systematically collects and reports data on all aspects of faculty effort.

A comprehensive workload system is a large undertaking in both its development and maintenance. It requires significant effort on the part of both the faculty and the administration. Two cautions are important here. First, throughout the workload literature, authors caution about imposing workload measures on the faculty without their involvement and support (Stecklein, 1961). Stated more succinctly, "faculty members dislike and distrust (outside) studies of their work habits" (Yuker, 1984, p. 24). Faculty were more likely to cooperate in workload studies if they believed the studies would provide data that were useful to their departments and that the departments could benefit from the results (Yuker, 1984). A second caution: if workload measures become too detailed and are used for resource allocations without consideration of other judgmental factors, faculty may begin to "work to the measures" without regard to the impact of the actions on the quality of their department.

University of Connecticut System. There are very few examples of institutionwide systems in the literature. Information on the University of Connecticut system summarized here comes from a report prepared in 1993 by the provost's office, *Toward the 21st Century: A Model for Academic Planning and Evaluation.* The Connecticut system is designed to evaluate departmental productivity through the efforts of the faculty. In the executive summary of the report, their system is described as "a unique model . . . that allows each academic unit to set goals consistent with the University's overarching goals, to evaluate itself with respect to these (unit) goals, and in concert with the administration to plan their achievements" (University of Connecticut, 1993, p. i). Later in the introduction, the report notes that the model is not intended as a replacement for judgment for administrators, but as a systematic way to provide information to those responsible for making decisions.

The model is designed to quantify scholarship, teaching, and service activities of the faculty and summarize these data in a series of easily understood measures. The model evaluation process begins with data from two sources: central university data and data collected from the faculty within each department. The departments are responsible for compiling most of the data each year. An academic planning committee reviews the data, helps develop the performance targets, and reviews the overall evaluation model process for effectiveness. Once the data and profiles have been reviewed by the units, they are forwarded to the dean and provost for use in assessment and planning activities.

The University of Connecticut system collects and reports information in four categories of departmental performance: centrality to mission, scholarship, teaching, and service. Within these four general categories, the model reports scores on ten dimensions, shown in the first column of Table 6.2. Subdimension scores are combined to form dimension scores for each unit. The third column on the table below lists the title for each dimension on the graphic profile presented later in this section.

Most of the data used for the departmental profiles come from the academic departments themselves. The University of Connecticut uses a standardized annual report format to collect data from each faculty member. A standard format is important because it ensures that all data elements are defined the same for the various units, comparable data are collected longitudinally for historical comparisons, and all faculty are included in the data collection effort.

Departments are the smallest unit of analysis in the Connecticut system. Departmental productivity is calculated and described by scores on ten dimensions and the results are graphed for easy understanding. Departmental performance target scores are also specified for the ten dimensions. Figure 6.1 is an example of a unit profile that compares actual performance with predetermined targets. The system is not designed or intended to provide data on the performance of individual faculty members.

Table 6.2. Departmental Evaluation Dimensions

Categories and Dimensions Centrality	Examples	Title in Profile Graph
Degree of centrality of that type of unit to all universities	Number of peers with this type of unit	State
Degree of centrality of unit to mission	n/a	Mission
Scholarship		
Creative productivity	Publications, performances	Productivity
Scholarly reputation	Editorships, officers, awards	Reputation
External funding	Applications, awards, direct costs	Funding
Teaching		
Undergraduate	SAT, GPA, degree ratio, awards	Undergraduate
Graduate	GRE, GPA, degree ratio, awards	Graduate
Service		
To the university	Committees and administrative jobs	University
To the state and community	Service, memberships, consults	State/Local
To the nation	Consults, professional groups	National

Source: University of Connecticut, 1993, pp. 36–39.

Other Workload Measurement Considerations

In concluding, three additional points must be raised: using the department as the focus of analysis and reporting, integrating workload measurement and reporting with other related processes at work concurrently within the institution, and including measures of quality in the analysis.

To this point, the discussion has focused on data related to individual faculty members. Individual faculty have individual interests and plans for their professional development. Some prefer teaching and others prefer research. A strong case can be made that institutional reporting and analysis of workload data be done at a level no lower than the department. In his 1961 book *How to Measure Faculty Work Load,* John E. Stecklein observed that analysis of faculty workload should be based on the following:

> average (faculty) work load data, obtained periodically for each department or each college, (to serve as) as a topic of discussion between faculty

Figure 6.1. Unit Profile Showing Actual and Target Performance Levels

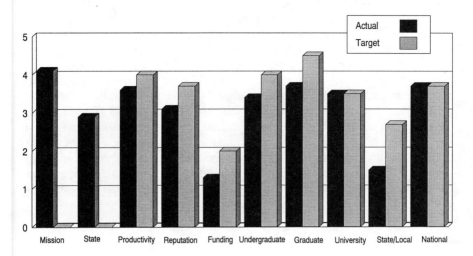

Source: University of Connecticut, 1993, p. 29.

and administrators. Consideration should be given to whether faculty emphasis, in terms of average time spent, is consistent with the stated purposes of the institution or department. For example, if a department or college faculty decide that its resources should be devoted one-half to instruction, and one-sixth to research, public services, and student services, these over-all proportions of faculty time may be maintained approximately (by each faculty) without setting them as a standard load for every faculty member. The departmental functional goals can be met by balance rather than uniformity. [Stecklein, 1961, pp. 35–36]

Another strong reason for establishing the department as the unit of reporting and analysis is the collaborative nature of most faculty work. In many disciplines, collaboration is the standard method of research and publication. When considered from the perspective of the curriculum as a whole, a case can be made that the instruction delivered by the department also be evaluated as a highly collaborative product.

Development of the workload measures should be coordinated with related activities that may be ongoing at the institution. Especially important would be coordination with any discussions of faculty roles and rewards, strategic planning, or mandatory reporting to state administrative or oversight organizations. Here, again, IR offices are in an ideal position to contribute to the coordination of such related planning and reporting activities.

A faculty workload measurement process should be used to document what the institution produces. At the same time, it can also provide useful data to chairs and deans for individual faculty evaluation. Collection of systematic evaluation data, in conjunction with predetermined performance standards, is at the heart of the current discussions on faculty roles and rewards. A faculty workload system, developed in conjunction with a review of roles and rewards, can support both the information needs of the institution and the needs of the faculty, chairs, and deans for individual performance reviews.

Finally, workload measures described throughout the literature focus exclusively on measures of quantity. This is in sharp contrast to the calls for more attention to quality, both from inside and outside of higher education. Clearly, measures of quality do exist. Sources include reviews of performance (possibly linked to roles and rewards discussions), program accreditation reports, peer reviews of research proposals and publications, student evaluations of teaching, and departmental and school evaluations of contributions to the unit and the institution. Although including such measures may be controversial, their inclusion adds a dimension to faculty workload that cannot be captured by measures of units produced.

Conclusion

This chapter has outlined several methods that have been applied to the measurement of faculty course loads or workloads. In the long run, choices for the methods to be used will be determined by the information needs of the institution; the data, computer tools, and staff resources available; the interest of the academic administration; and, ultimately, the support and cooperation of the faculty. The key to implementing faculty workload measurement is to keep the plan in balance so that it produces as much desired information as possible without exceeding the resources or capacity of the institution to maintain and support the process or the patience and support of the faculty.

References

"A College Education at What Cost?" *Richmond Times-Dispatch,* September 12–16, 1993.

An Overview of Results from the Virginia Faculty Survey. Survey Research Laboratory of Virginia Commonwealth University. June 27, 1991.

Braxton, J. M., and Bayer, A. E. "Assessing Faculty Scholarly Performance." In J. W. Creswell (ed.), *Measuring Faculty Research Performance.* New Directions for Institutional Research, no. 50. San Francisco: Jossey-Bass, 1986.

Colorado State University Office of Planning and Budgets. *Comparative Staffing Units as a Measure of University Instructional Workload,* Second edition. Fort Collins: Colorado State University, 1975.

Heydinger, R. B., and Simsek, H. *An Agenda for Reshaping Faculty Productivity.* Denver: State Higher Education Executive Officers, 1992.

Hopper, L. K. *Faculty Workload: Implementing a Strategy for Assessing Faculty Utilization.* Paper presented at the Association for Institutional Research (AIR) Annual Meeting, May 1992.

Jordan, S. M., and Layzell, D. T. *A Case Study of Faculty Workload Issues in Arizona: Implications for State Higher Education Policy.* Denver: State Higher Education Executive Officers, 1992.

"New Data Base Is Intended to Find Academic Partners for Businesses." *Chronicle of Higher Education,* August 11, 1993, pp. 19–20.

Shull, E. H. *Quantitative Assessment of Faculty Workloads.* Chicago: Association for the Study of Higher Education, 1984.

Stecklein, J. E. *How to Measure Faculty Workload.* Washington, D.C.: American Council on Education, 1961.

University of Connecticut Office of the Provost. *Toward the 21st Century: A Model for Academic Planning and Evaluation.* Storrs: University of Connecticut, Jan. 1993, pp. 36–39.

University of Maine System Office. *UMSserve, University of Maine System Public Service Resource Network.* Unpublished summary report, May 26, 1993.

Yuker, H. *Faculty Workload: Research, Theory and Interpretation,* ASHE-ERIC Higher Education Research Report #10. Washington, D.C.: Association for the Study of Higher Education, 1984.

LLOYD BYRD, JR. is a senior institutional research and evaluation associate in the office of institutional research and evaluation at Virginia Commonwealth University, Richmond.

Changes in government financing of social programs, global economic and social developments, changes in attitudes, and developments in information technology may well transform the role of faculty in the next century.

Beyond Faculty Workload: External Forces Affecting the Future of the Professoriat

James R. Mingle, Richard B. Heydinger

Higher education in the United States has been transformed throughout its history by forces external to the academy. In the latter part of the nineteenth century, the need to industrialize America led to the shift from colonial, church-related colleges to public land-grant institutions comprising a collection of professional colleges. Following World War II, the need to preserve an effective, war-related research enterprise led to the creation of the federal policy that has driven our research agenda for the past four decades. At the same time, higher education institutions were pushed by the public to educate a large demographic cohort of returning GIs. This democratizing force was accelerated by the civil rights movement of the 1960s, which opened wide the doors of colleges and universities to minority groups previously denied access.

In this chapter, we posit that, once again, external forces will have the greatest impact on the academy and particularly on the roles faculty play. Four external conditions or trends, which are already being felt and are likely to accelerate over the next decade, will drive these changes:

Changes in governmental financing of the social agenda

Global changes, specifically population growth and environmental degradation in developing countries

Growth and interest in privatization and the transformation of public governance structures and the resulting increased competition in higher education

Developments in information technology

NEW DIRECTIONS FOR INSTITUTIONAL RESEARCH, no. 83, Fall 1994 © Jossey-Bass Publishers

These forces will reshape the form and substance of higher education in the next several years and have significant implications for faculty work. In the discussion that follows, we speculate on what those implications might be.

In contrast to previous times, the external forces pushing on the academy today are viewed by higher education as constraining, not expanding forces. Interestingly, this is not true of public policy makers. From their perspective, these external forces will push higher education toward controlling its costs while extending its reach. In today's parlance, this is the expectation to do more with less.

Changes in Governmental Financing of Social Functions

Over the past decade, we have gone through a revolution in attitudes about public finance. Cutting across all of our policies has loomed the federal deficit and a growing skepticism about the value of government-sponsored programs. In higher education, our sense of neglect has grown acute and is only slightly mollified by the return of economic growth in 1993. We also reason that if we bide our time, once again we will be the darlings of state legislators and congress and that the golden years (are those still the 1960s?) will return.

We suspect that such a return to favor is not going to happen. An objective look at the 1980s reveals some sobering news. During the past decade, growth in revenue from all sources—federal, state, and private—grew significantly faster than the economy as a whole and significantly faster than enrollment (Hauptman, 1992). Halsted (1993) reported that we ended the decade of the 1980s with higher rates of support per student, even after adjusting for inflation, than we began. Certainly, many public institutions suffered significant declines in state support during the recession of the early 1990s, but many made up for those cutbacks by raising tuition. The California Higher Education Policy Center (1994) reports that California institutions, despite state cutbacks, have more money per student than they did before the recession in California began, primarily because of tuition increases and the decision to limit enrollment.

Interestingly, the level of taxation, considering all sources, has remained relatively constant over the past decade, although the mix has changed significantly and has had differential impact on classes of individuals (Snell, 1993). The Republicans' reputation for cutting taxes and Democrats' reputation for raising taxes is a myth, especially when we look at all levels of government. Apparently there is a relatively constant capacity or willingness of the public to support governmental programs. Cuts in income taxes provided the opportunity to raise social security taxes; cuts in federal taxes provided taxation opportunities at other levels of government. Now cuts in property taxes are likely to open the door for new state taxes.

Although the tax revolt may be a myth, the source and use of these taxes is under considerable change. Much of this new taxation, especially at the state and federal levels, has gone to pay the price of demographics, namely, the aging of our population as reflected in rising health care and social security costs (Gold, 1991). Other social costs, such as crime, also are growing, but these are minor compared to the costs of aging. The escalation of these aging costs will continue as the U.S. population grows older over the next twenty years.

The effect of these changing state priorities on higher education will continue. We have been a shrinking priority for some time. Even through the growth years of the 1980s, our share of revenue declined, especially our state government share. Halsted (1993) notes that "higher education has declined from a peak 8.3 percent of state and local government budgets in 1979–80 to 6.3 percent today" (p. 26). Masked by the economic growth of the 1980s (appropriations continued to grow in absolute terms because of increased tax collections), our relative standing became readily apparent during the recession of the early 1990s. By 1994, the trend had moderated, but is likely to continue due to a number of factors, including structural problems with tax systems, especially at the state level. For example, our tax systems no longer capture growth even when it occurs, primarily because we depend so heavily on sales taxes, which typically exempt most services (Snell, 1993).

The biggest change affecting higher education finance over the past decade may have been the change in attitudes about tuition. Interestingly, public polls do not show the same concern about quality in higher education, but there is great anxiety about the price (Immerwahr and Farkas, 1993). In fact, a college education has become the new national symbol of outrageous expense in the media. For example, witness advertisements for investment firms and others who want to play on this national concern.

This is already moderating the tuition increases that colleges are willing to implement, especially private colleges. Simultaneously, state legislators and the public are objecting to enrollment limitations. This leaves little choice but to consider more cost-effective ways to deliver higher education.

Ironically, arguments about its value have undermined higher education's claim on the public treasury. By citing the economic benefits—in the form of lifetime earnings added by a college degree—higher education leaders have reinforced the idea that these benefits accrue primarily to the individual, and by implication, not to society. Thus, they implicitly argue that the cost should increasingly be borne by the individual. As a friend once remarked, "The state of California sent my daughter to medical school at a ridiculously low price. We will always be grateful."

From this perspective, we draw two conclusions. The change in public attitude about private benefits compared to public benefits is relatively permanent. Second, given the structural and demographic forces facing state and federal governments, higher education's share of tax revenues is likely to continue to decline. At best, higher education will match, not exceed, growth rates for the economy as a whole. The result will be continuous pressure on higher education to improve its cost effectiveness and productivity.

As a result we can continue to expect public pressure about teaching loads, calendars, and general concern that instruction is being neglected in favor of research. Expect continued legislative pressure on institutions to increase teaching loads and to constrain tenure granting, either directly through tightened criteria and review or indirectly through the hiring of part-timers and adjuncts. Institutions also will continue to examine the curriculum to see whether low-enrollment courses at upper-division levels can be pared. Such moves should not be surprising. Higher education is a labor-intensive enterprise. Faculty salaries constitute the second largest expenditure in the budget of many states, after teacher salaries. Furthermore, the flexible working conditions and job security afforded most regular faculty are at great variance with those of the population as a whole, even with other professions. Thus, as Margaret Miller points out in Chapter One of this volume, public patience has worn thin.

Economic Competitiveness, Global Population, and Environmental Changes

In an essay titled "Government and Higher Education," Patrick Callan (1993) reminds us how much the agenda of government, and more specifically the agenda of governors, became a force for change in the 1980s. In earlier decades, the federal government was the force for change. In the 1980s, the state-led agenda was focused (some might say obsessed) on making the educational systems a part of the economic development strategies of states. In answer to the question, "What has gotten the governors' attention [to education]?," then Tennessee Governor Lamar Alexander responded, "Jobs. More than anything, it is the threat to the jobs of the people who elect us" (National Governors Association, 1986, p. 5).

This concern with global economic competitiveness continues to dominate the national scene and state agendas. To compete and win in the global economy (to borrow President Clinton's phrase) remains the single national goal that unites Democrats and Republicans. The impact on higher education can be seen in the tremendous interest in and demand for vocational and professional education that leads quickly to graduation and employment.

Yet it has not always been so, nor will it always be so. The national agenda will shift with global developments, and with that shift national policy (and attitudes) toward higher education will change. The results are difficult to predict. The globalization of the economy and of communications is likely to further separate faculty from their communities and their states, which are still a significant source of their financial support. In the long term, such arrangements seem nonsustainable, especially for major research universities. A faculty operating globally and supported locally seems to be headed for trouble.

The issues that drive our agenda may also shift dramatically. Paul Kennedy (1993), in his book *Preparing for the Twenty-First Century,* suggests that the spillover effects of population explosion in developing nations—environmental degradation and the disintegration of nation-states—will dominate the attention of our children and grandchildren. The leading effects of these events are already apparent in states such as Florida, Texas, and California where social services, including educational institutions, are being overwhelmed by immigrants and the public backlash is growing.

What will be the effects of this interaction of an aging and affluent American population with young and increasingly poor, desperate, and often criminal countries? One possibility is to retreat behind the barricades of walled communities and fenced borders. Another is a turn inward to concerns about spirituality and a search for meaning in this chaos. Still another, more optimistic answer is Al Gore's vision of an American society engaged with the world's problems and coming up with solutions to its environmental problems. Whatever the turn of America, one can expect it to be felt directly in the academy—in its curricula, its structure, and its goals. The dividing lines between society and the academy will again become a much debated topic, as it was 100 years ago when we debated the role of higher education in "agriculture and the mechanic arts."

As for the need for various types of faculty expertise, one can imagine a number of different scenarios. Humanities faculty may find themselves in great demand among an aging baby-boomer cohort concerned with the meaning of life and spirituality. One can distinctly foresee a growing legion of criminal justice experts to advise us on our growing security concerns, along with experts on political disintegration, transnational migration, and other geopolitical concerns. Given the continuing environmental degradation, one anticipates a host of environmental regulators, engineers, and cleanup experts.

Privatization, Enterprises, and Increased Competition

The Pew Higher Education Roundtable (1994), in the essay "To Dance with Change," cited the press of privatization as one of the major forces that will reshape higher education in the years ahead. This will come as a surprise to many private colleges, which have been so neglected by policy makers in recent years. But the atmosphere is changing. In the past, private higher education has been regarded by policy makers as a problem, something they were being asked to save from financial bankruptcy and closure. Increasingly, however, especially in states facing growing demand and limited public support, private institutions are being viewed as a solution, or at least as an excuse not to invest further in public higher education.

Many existing private liberal arts colleges, however, are not well-positioned to take advantage of emerging markets. They are not nimble enough to respond quickly to a rapidly changing world. Many are still provider-driven rather than customer-focused. Thus, we will see entrepreneurial, profit-making institutions delivering courses via satellite and Internet, or we will see large, aggressive, and prestigious public universities or consortia delivering programs and courses across state lines. We may also see moves to privatize public institutions, or at least parts of public institutions, such as professional schools.

The movement to reinvent government and new private sector management concepts are also affecting the activities and governance structures of public institutions. Armajani, Heydinger, and Hutchinson (1994) have proposed an enterprise model for the organization of public higher education. In this approach, major functions are organized as separate public enterprises. For example, a facilities enterprise would own, manage, and maintain the state's higher education facilities, with their customers being the educational enterprises. The same would be true of libraries and computing.

Armajani and colleagues (1994) also suggest that teaching enterprises could replace existing departments. In this case, groups of faculty organized around a discipline or a delivery style would contract with various educational enterprises to provide particular services. Teaching faculty would have the freedom to govern the enterprise according to the values and norms they find most acceptable. The educational enterprise itself would focus exclusively on delivering high-quality educational services to the student and would not be concerned about the governance of the educational enterprise.

In such a model, policies focused on means (such as specific teaching loads or student–faculty ratios) are replaced by a system driven by performance measures and customer satisfaction. In this approach, the costs and the revenues of each enterprise and program are made known. Institutions can continue to subsidize programs that do not "carry their own weight," but this is made more explicit than in the current system of hidden subsidies and unknown program costs. Faculty may also find themselves working for multiple institutions and clients. Workload and employment contracts will need to be adjusted accordingly.

Changes also will occur at the state and system levels. The virtues of competition may well replace the old values of placing constraints on competitive forces. Much of state policy in higher education is built around unnecessary duplication and the desire to protect in-state public institutions from competition from private providers or public out-of-state providers. In other words, higher education coordinating boards have played the role of negotiators of trade barriers (in the name of quality) in order to protect the native farmers from the destructive forces of the marketplace.

These policy assumptions will be severely tested in the emerging higher education marketplace. Technology is rapidly putting an end to the historic relationship between cost and access. Additional access in the form of additional delivery sites or nodes on the Internet becomes essentially a no-cost addition. In fact, to make the large front-end investments cost-effective, numbers and locations must grow substantially. The average cost for a single course development in the British Open University is more than $1 million, but the average course enrollment reaches 200,000 students. Thus, due to economies of scale, there will be a strong push by these providers to expand their enrollment, thereby spreading their fixed costs over a larger group and reducing their costs per student.

In short, the competitive environment in higher education is likely to dramatically increase in the years to come. Alternative providers, both state-sponsored and privately sponsored, are likely to compete with traditional higher education systems. Ironically, some of the most intense competition may come from traditional providers in other states. From the perspective of the consumer and the public policy maker, this will be positive. Competition will expand access and lower costs. However, it could significantly change the roles of faculty.

The University of Phoenix, a for-profit degree-granting institution, may well be the prototype of the future. Courses aimed primarily at working adults are taught exclusively by adjunct faculty who are working professionals. Wages for these instructors are quite low. Curriculum is developed centrally by discipline experts working on a project contract basis, augmented by a few full-time staff, all of whom are well-compensated.

Market-driven compensation policies, even for traditional faculty roles, could be adopted. Heydinger and Simsek (1992) suggest that institutions adopt compensation policies that are essentially base-plus systems, not unlike the way in which faculty in medical schools are currently compensated. Such an approach also would require a change in the way in which faculty are compensated for funded research. This model suggests that compensation be more directly related to a discrete set of services provided by faculty, rather than the current system, in which a fixed annual salary is assumed and only time allocations are negotiated.

The increasingly competitive environment also is likely to change dramatically the way in which we fund higher education, with the biggest impact on state universities. In the future, it will be difficult for states to subsidize access for one set of providers (public university systems) while excluding all others. The result could be voucher systems in which the large majority of public support is carried by students, while institutional support is reserved for the purchase of particular services on behalf of state and federal governments.

We have a limited voucher system operating now at the federal level that has spawned a wide set of providers in vocational education, many of them low quality. The system also has apparently escalated costs to the maximum borrowing limits, another major problem with the approach. To overcome these weaknesses, a number of changes are needed. First, we must improve the knowledge and sophistication of consumers (namely, students). This could be done through expanded public information systems and independent or private entrepreneurial companies that report to students on the performance of institutions, especially their performance in helping students meet externally developed standards and pass licensing exams. These organizations, which

Armajani, Heydinger, and Hutchinson (1994) call learning connections, might well replace the student service, placement, and counseling offices of colleges and universities.

The second change that must be made is in student aid policy. Rather than striving to meet unmet needs, we must index our subsidies to something external to the institution (such as personal income or government assessment of reasonable costs). At the same time, policy makers will see deregulation as a means for increasing competition, which in turn will hold down costs. The parallels with health care are hauntingly familiar!

Taken together, the forces of privatization, enterprise-oriented public systems, new faculty reward structures, and an even more competitive environment are ingredients of a rich recipe for change. Folded into this recipe will be perhaps the most significant change for education since the printing press: information technology.

Developments in Information Technology

It is impossible to witness the dramatic changes in information technology without expecting them to affect higher education. In many ways they already have, especially in research. The Internet has facilitated the emergence of a global, horizontal university connecting faculty to their peers around the world.

Although we have this emerging infrastructure for research, no such infrastructure exists for instruction. Some analysts expect that a set of national institutions delivering televised instruction via satellite and cable will emerge. A few such institutions and consortia already exist. The Internet appears to hold far more potential, however, especially in engaging students interactively. There are early indications that significant changes in the teaching and learning process may be around the corner. In some courses, for example, students go on-line to meet with fellow students from around the world. They may share experiences from a cross-cultural perspective or work collectively to complete a specific assignment. If the appropriate protocols and curriculum standards can be developed, software companies, publishers, and testing companies may find it financially feasible to invest in a national or global learning infrastructure.

The implications of a sophisticated, interactive, Internet-based learning system are potentially very substantial. William Graves (1994) of the University of North Carolina, Chapel Hill and consultant to EDUCOM, notes that the "prevailing method of quality assurance in higher education starts with the final grade, which is typically dependent on examinations administered by instructors" (p. 7). As Graves notes, having instructors as evaluators has one great advantage: it puts standard setting in the hands of the content expert. However, it also has a number of disadvantages that cause policy makers and the public to be highly critical of the current system. Because it is a local form of quality assurance, it inhibits transfer of credit, not only at the course level but at the degree level. More important to the cost dilemmas discussed earlier, this method of quality assurance greatly constrains section size "unless the instructor opts for some form of 'automated' testing, such as machine-graded multiple choice exams, often at the expense of quality" (Graves, 1994). Keep in mind that section size more than any other factor determines instructional cost.

The other great weakness of the current delivery system, which is dominated by the lecture form of instruction, is its inflexibility. It is adjustable neither to the learning advantages or deficiencies of individual students nor to the constraints of time and place. In contrast, the Internet is completely flexible to time and place and, through sophisticated software, to the learning needs of individuals.

Learning software is being developed by individual faculty in the same cottage industry style that dominates higher education, but a national infrastructure as described by Graves would depend on both national protocols as well as national curriculum standards. In the view of EDUCOM, these standards would be developed by the discipline societies, in concert with the private sector—publishers, software companies, cable companies, and utilities. States and the federal government would ideally be partners, although we are less optimistic about their capacity and willingness to make these investments. Without these protocols and standards, Graves believes these investments will not take place.

Some of the academy will fear and oppose any government involvement in the establishment of such standards. However, such fears are unwarranted. We expect these standards to emerge from individuals and from leading national institutions, rather than from governmental entities. (In this respect, we make an important distinction between national and federal standards.) All of these scenarios would require a significant change in the role of faculty and imply new definitions of faculty productivity. Faculty are likely to see their very diffuse and diverse set of roles become more specialized. One can conceive of the following specializations:

A large number of mentors, tutors, and navigators of the Internet assisting students who are engaged in interactive learning. Rather than being the intermediary who sorts and interprets knowledge for the student, the faculty member is the guide in a game of individual discovery. From "sage on the stage," the faculty member moves to "mentor at the monitor." This is a curious return to the origins of faculty, but it is an Internet address sitting on the other end of the log.

The demand for a significant, but not large, number of curriculum specialists who move from working on textbooks to working with discipline societies, software companies, testing companies, and publishers on the protocols and standards needed for this new interactive curriculum.

A few highly visible performers, who are "on stage" either through televised instruction, CD-ROM, or the information superhighway, using the full range of multimedia materials. Finally we will have faculty (a small proportion perhaps) who are nationally recognized for their outstanding teaching.

A significant but declining number of faculty who may not be engaged in instruction at all but in research, service, and contract activities with paying clients outside the institution. These individuals will essentially be entrepreneurs who live by their wits, and are compensated accordingly. In many ways, the daily activities of this cohort will not change markedly from today. Today they are the 15–25 percent of productive researchers who are currently serving in research universities.

Depending on one's perspective, this scenario is either enlightened or horrifying. Many faculty, not surprisingly, will resist with great force the idea of no longer serving as an intermediary between students and knowledge. Experience in other fields suggests that they will be successful. Kennedy (1993), for example, believes that social and demographic conditions in the United States are not right for the wide-scale use of robotics. Only societies with labor shortages, such as Japan and Germany, are making any progress in the application of robotics in the manufacturing sector. For example, in law and health care, the strategy has been to replace expensively trained and well-paid personnel with less well-trained and less expensive paraprofessionals. To some degree, we have done this in higher education with the use of part-time faculty, adjuncts, and teaching assistants (usually not less well-trained but rather surplus labor). But this is still not substituting a "learning machine" for a teacher.

Other interesting dilemmas arise. For example, institutional leaders and state policy makers could be faced with vexing choices in this new technology era unbounded by the constraints of time or place. If you could have the best engineering faculty in the country deliver courses at your location via telecommunications, would you want to go to the expense of hiring your own faculty? It is also not clear whether students are prepared or interested in such a "disintermediated" system. Interactive learning, whether on the job or through the Internet, requires a certain level of competence, self-discipline, and motivation, traits often missing in today's students, according to faculty. Critics of the new technology often conjure up the image of the small colonial college with considerable student–faculty interaction. In telling reactions to the technology scenario recently advanced by Robert Zemsky of the Pew Higher Education Roundtable (1994), administrators from small colleges argued that basic intellectual skills developed by a liberal education cannot be taught in this way. "Many rite-of-passage students today are not ready or willing learners," noted one academic dean (p. 4B).

Such observations, of course, are contradictory. If they are not prepared for interactive software they probably are not prepared for the Socratic method so revered by the liberal arts. Only a small percentage of students have ever wanted or benefited from this small college experience. Probably a more legitimate comparison is whether interactive software can and should replace the lecture hall.

More important to the question of implementation is not student capacity but student demand. Certainly, much about the traditional college market has nothing to do with learning and everything to do with that rite of passage spoken of by the academic dean. We expect the weakest market demand for a technology-driven curriculum to be found among traditional students, and the strongest demand among working professionals. After all, much of adult learning is already self-directed.

Another constraint on this information technology model is the exclusive franchise colleges have on the credential itself. This franchise is protected by states, accrediting bodies, and, to a lesser degree, the federal government. However, the willingness to end or significantly transform this credential function is in the wind. It is in the wind in the form of performance standards at the K–12 level and in the increasing emphasis on student outcomes in higher education.

From the perspective of state coordinating boards or even accrediting bodies, there may be little or no inherent interest in one particular academic process over another. Acceptable and maybe even superior outcomes in student learning may emerge from these new delivery systems. If this occurs, states will be hard-pressed to dictate through their regulatory and funding policies a preference for a certain kind of institution or traditional credential. Learning outcomes may become the foundation for our quality assurance and accountability systems.

As this happens, state interest in the vertical university as an organized bureaucracy may decline while its interest in supporting the horizontal university could increase. This transition will be especially difficult for state policy makers who are interested in investing in institutions as a representation of the state persona. However, if a significant proportion of legislators overcome this reluctance, it could easily mean a dramatic change in funding strategies. Already there is considerable interest and some action to fund performance. We also are seeing new investment strategies in the form of technology councils that direct funds for cross-cutting activities, and administrative and purchasing consortia to build interinstitutional networks and cut costs.

As student options multiply and if learning outcomes become the foundation for quality assurance and accountability, the focus for funding will shift from the institution to the student. Policy makers will be more likely to provide support directly to the student, in the form of a voucher, and let them decide among competing learning opportunities, all of which exceed the state's specified threshold of learning quality. In this scenario, the state would have information on outcomes available for prospective students. In this way, the higher education consumer of the twenty-first century may be a much more informed shopper than today's matriculant.

Thus, information technology is a potentially potent force that could break the logjam of institutional reengineering. Its capacities offer institutional designers, entrepreneurs, and public officials many levers for change. Its implications go beyond flexible, interactive curriculum to include new funding strategies and entirely new, horizontal forms of interinstitutional degrees.

The Interaction of These External Forces

As we have attempted to demonstrate, each of these four external forces holds implications for the future of higher education. Yet when these forces begin to come together, a much different paradigm may emerge. Borrowing from music composition, we view changes in the financing of public functions and the effect of global changes as the bass clef of the symphony we call higher education. Financing mechanisms and societal conditions form the rhythm and the background beat. As in a good symphony, we often do not notice their presence, but they are always there. They are the framework within which the symphony is played.

Changes in information technology, privatization, public enterprises, and increased competition will determine the melody or the treble clef of higher education activities in the next few decades. It is the melody that is most memorable, and it is the melody that people typically hum. Yet it is a combination of the steady progress of the bass clef with the variations and syncopation in the melody that will determine whether we like the new symphony of higher education. The music is being composed. All of us working in higher education have an opportunity to help compose the new score.

References

Armajani, B., Heydinger, R. B., and Hutchinson, P. *A Model for the Reinvented Higher Education System*. Denver: The Education Commission of the States and the State Higher Education Executive Officers, 1994.

California Higher Education Policy Center. *Time for Decision*. San Jose: California Higher Education Policy Center, March 1994.

Callan, P. M. "Government and Higher Education." In A. Levine (ed.), *Higher Learning in America, 1980–2000*. Baltimore: The Johns Hopkins University Press, 1993.

Gold, S. D. *Changes in State Government Finances in the 1980s*. Albany: State University of New York, 1991.

Graves, W. H. "Toward a National Learning Infrastructure." Unpublished draft paper by EDUCOM, March 27, 1994.

Halsted, K. *State Profiles: Financing Public Higher Education 1978 to 1993*. Washington, D.C.: Research Associates of Washington, 1993.

Hauptman, A. M. *The Economic Prospects for American Higher Education*. Washington, D.C.: Association of Governing Boards, 1992.

Heydinger, R. B., and Simsek, H. *An Agenda for Reshaping Faculty Productivity*. Denver: State Higher Education Executive Officers, 1992.

Immerwahr, J., and Farkas, S. *The Closing Gateway: Californians Consider Their Higher Education System*. San Jose: California Higher Education Policy Center, 1993.

Kennedy, P. M. *Preparing for the Twenty-First Century*. New York: Random House, 1993.

National Governors' Association. *Time for Results*. Washington, D.C.: National Governors' Association, 1986.

The Pew Higher Education Roundtable. "To Dance With Change." *Policy Perspectives,* 1994, 5 (3).

Snell, R. D. (ed.). *Financing State Government in the 1990s.* Washington, D.C.: National Conference of State Legislatures and the National Governors' Association, 1993.

JAMES R. MINGLE is executive director of the State Higher Education Executive Officers in Denver, Colorado.

RICHARD B. HEYDINGER is executive director of the Alliance for Higher Education Strategies and a partner in The Public Strategies Group, Inc., St. Paul, Minnesota.

INDEX

Ordering Information

NEW DIRECTIONS FOR INSTITUTIONAL RESEARCH is a series of paperback books that provides planners and administrators in all types of academic institutions with guidelines in such areas as resource coordination, information analysis, program evaluation, and institutional management. Books in the series are published quarterly in spring, summer, fall, and winter and are available for purchase by subscription as well as by single copy.

SUBSCRIPTIONS for 1994 cost $47.00 for individuals (a savings of 25 percent over single-copy prices) and $62.00 for institutions, agencies, and libraries. Please do not send institutional checks for personal subscriptions. Standing orders are accepted.

SINGLE COPIES cost $15.95 when payment accompanies order. (California, New Jersey, New York, and Washington, D.C., residents please include appropriate sales tax.) Billed orders will be charged postage and handling.

DISCOUNTS FOR QUANTITY ORDERS are available. Please write to the address below for information.

ALL ORDERS must include either the name of an individual or an official purchase order number. Please submit your order as follows:
Subscriptions: specify series and year subscription is to begin
Single copies: include individual title code (such as IR78)

MAIL ALL ORDERS TO:
Jossey-Bass Publishers
350 Sansome Street
San Francisco, CA 94104-1342

FOR SUBSCRIPTION SALES OUTSIDE OF THE UNITED STATES, CONTACT: any international subscription agency or Jossey-Bass directly.

Statement of Ownership, Management and Circulation
(Required by 39 U.S.C. 3685)

1A. Title of Publication: NEW DIRECTIONS FOR INSTITUTIONAL RESEARCH
1B. Publication No.: 0 2 7 1 0 5 7 9
2. Date of Filing: 9/26/94
3. Frequency of Issue: Quarterly
3A. No. of Issues Published Annually: Four (4)
3B. Annual Subscription Price: $47.00 (personal) $62.00 (institutional)

4. Complete Mailing Address of Known Office of Publication: 350 Sansome Street, 5th Flr, San Francisco, CA 94104-1342 (San Francisco Cnty)

5. Complete Mailing Address of the Headquarters of General Business Offices of the Publisher: (above address)

6. Full Names and Complete Mailing Address of Publisher, Editor, and Managing Editor
Publisher: Jossey-Bass Inc., Publishers (above address)
Editor: Patrick T. Terenzini, Ctr for the Study of Higher Educ, Pennsylvania State Univ, 403 S. Allen St. Ste 104, University Park, PA 16801-5202
Managing Editor: Lynn D. Luckow, President, Jossey-Bass Inc., Publishers (address above)

7. Owner:
Simon & Schuster — PO Box 1172, Englewood Cliffs, NJ 07632-1172

8. Known Bondholders, Mortgagees, and Other Security Holders:
same as above — same as above

9. For Completion by Nonprofit Organizations
Has Not Changed During Preceding 12 Months

10. Extent and Nature of Circulation	Average No. Copies Each Issue During Preceding 12 Months	Actual No. Copies of Single Issue Published Nearest to Filing Date
A. Total No. Copies	2,010	2,150
B. Paid and/or Requested Circulation 1. Sales through dealers and carriers, street vendors and counter sales	451	512
2. Mail Subscription	762	716
C. Total Paid and/or Requested Circulation	1,213	1,228
D. Free Distribution by Mail, Carrier or Other Means	66	66
E. Total Distribution	1,279	1,294
F. Copies Not Distributed 1. Office use, left over, unaccounted, spoiled after printing	731	856
2. Return from News Agents	0	0
G. TOTAL	2,010	2,150

11. I certify that the statements made by me above are correct and complete
Larry Ishii, Vice President

PS Form 3526, January 1991